THE REAL WORK

THE REAL WORK

INTERVIEWS & TALKS 1964–1979

GARY SNYDER

Edited with an introduction by Wm. Scott McLean

A NEW DIRECTIONS BOOK

Manufactured in the United States of America
New Directions books are printed on acid-free paper.
First published clothbound and as New Directions Paperbook 499 in 1980
Published simultaneously in Canada by Penguin Books Canada Limited

Library of Congress Cataloging in Publication Data

Snyder, Gary.
   The real work.
   (A New Directions Book)
   1.   Snyder, Gary—Interviews.   2.   Poets, American—
20th century—Interviews.   I.   McLean, William Scott.
II.   Title.
PS3569.N88z473   1980   811'.54   79–27319
ISBN 0–8112–0760-9
ISBN 0–8112–0761-7 pbk.

New Directions Books are published for James Laughlin
by New Directions Publishing Corporation,
80 Eighth Avenue, New York 10011

SIXTH PRINTING

ACKNOWLEDGMENTS

Grateful acknowledgment is made to the editors and publishers of the following journals and magazines in which some of these interviews first appeared: *Berkeley Barb, City Miner Magazine* (Issue #12, P.O. Box 176, Berkeley, CA 94701), *East West Journal, Espejo* (Spring 1974, Vol. XII, No. 2, Southern Methodist University), *Field, Io/12* (Earth Geography Booklet No. 1), *Literary Times, New York Quarterly, The Ohio Review* (Vol. XVIII, No. 3), *Plucked Chicken, Road Apple Review,* and *Western Slopes Connection.*

Acknowledgment is also given to the following for the use of excerpts in the section "Some Further Angles": *Conversations: Christian and Buddhist* by Dom Aelred Graham (Copyright © 1968 by Dom Aelred Graham; reprinted by permission of Harcourt Brace Jovanovich, Inc.), *Mountain Gazette, Poetry Nippon* 21, *River Styx* 4 (1979), and *Wind Bell* (Vol. VIII, Nos. 1-2, Fall 1969, published by the Zen Center).

The editor would like to give special thanks to Peggy Fox of New Directions for her care in helping put this book together.

FOR KAI, GEN, AND DAVID

A NOTE FROM GARY SNYDER

I would like to thank the men and women who provided warm rooms and tea, and then posed questions and elicited information. This book is a product of the interaction of many minds. In particular I would like to acknowledge the creative and deliberate interviews by Peter Barry Chowka and Paul Geneson, interviews in the course of which I learned things.

Without the energy of my collaborator-editor, Scott McLean, these papers would have remained scattered through the periodicals. Thanks to Scott and Patricia McLean.

Finally I would like to thank the people who transcribe tapes. It's slow, tedious work, but without their labor, our attempts to capture the spirit of the moment and the freshness of the oral context, and then put it on paper, would come to naught.

CONTENTS

vironmental movement and minorities—Land Reform—
Science and technology—Energy technologies—Space
colonies—Reflections on the California Arts Council—
Governor Brown—Zen—Shamanism—Mahayana Bud-
dhism—Poetry and tradition—The printed word—Northern
California politics

INTRODUCTION

In 1969 Gary Snyder published a collection of journal excerpts, reviews, translations, and essays under the title *Earth House Hold*. The materials collected covered a fifteen-year period, spanning the years Snyder spent doing forest service lookout duty in the Cascade Mountains of Washington State (1952–53) to his marriage with Masa Uehara on Suwa-no-se Island in 1967.

Thematically and structurally the interviews and talks gathered in this volume complement and extend the positions taken in *Earth House Hold*. A line can be traced in the earlier prose collection from Snyder's first statements on poetics in the "Lookout's Journal" to the essay "Suwa-no-se Island and the Banyan Ashram," celebrating a sense of community that has been lost all too long. A similar line can be followed in *The Real Work,* from Snyder's comments on the complementary nature of inner and outer realities explored in his poetry to the talk "Poetry, Community, & Climax." But whereas the relationship between poetry and community was only sketched out in the later essays of *Earth House Hold,* it becomes the focal point early in this collection, as poetry is seen more and more by Snyder to be a binding force in the fabric of community life.

Gary Snyder's poetry has continued a tradition first pursued in late eighteenth-century Romantic thought and carried on in American literature most notably by Thoreau: a belief that the "outer and inner life correspond" and that poetry is "the self-consciousness of the universe," the voice of the universe reflecting on itself and on the interdependence of outer and inner nature. Poetry as "the seat of the soul"—the area where the inner world and the outer world touch, where they "interpenetrate" each other.[1]

But if Snyder's work follows this thread in European and American literature, the bases for his poetry lie elsewhere: in oral traditions of transmission, in Chinese and Japanese poetics, and in the ancient and worldwide sense of the Earth Goddess as inspirer of song.

Snyder's early work in *Riprap* was directed toward getting down to a flat surface reality, to break what William Carlos Williams called the "complicated ritualistic forms designed to separate the work from reality."[2] This attention to phenomena in order to discover poetic form in that reality was sharpened by the meditative teachings of Japanese and Chinese poets leading to mind before language and in what is now more than twenty-five years of Zen practice, a discipline which takes one "to *anything* direct—rocks or bushes or people" (*Earth House Hold,* 34). One of the keys to the poems in *The Back Country,* especially those in the section "Far East," is this turning to the "flat, concrete surface of 'things,' without bringing anything of imagination or intellect to bear on it."[3]

In reaching that "absolute bottom transparency," Snyder's meditative poetry has taken two directions. One is toward a short lyric that pushes up against an edge of silence, an ellipsis where the silence defines the form and substance. In a number of these poems ("Pine Tree Tops" is a good example) the texts represent "arrested phenomena," and the poems become, as Donald Wesling says in a related context, "like the 'objects' of modern physics, . . . at once product and process."[4] These poems are small "knots," "whorls in the grain," a bit of stored energy that draws the reader/listener at the end of the poem to follow out in his or her mind the pathways marked.

The second form Snyder's meditative poetry takes is the long poem that begins in the everyday world but then spirals up from that area, working on more mythological and archetypal levels. *Myths & Texts* (1960) has the movement of an elegy, going back and forth between the present and the past, as the poem follows various paths in history, in nature, in the world of work. We can best approach these poems in Snyder's terms of mind penetrating the different realms: "Now, we are both in, and outside, the world at once. The only place this can be is the *Mind*. Ah, what a poem. It is what is, completely, in the past, present, and future simultaneously, seeing being and being seen" (*Turtle Island,* 114). Pushed up hard against phenomena, in the smoky burn of the mind that leads up through an area described in the Hopi image of the smokehole that connects the worlds, Snyder's longer meditative poetry functions like a double mirror, showing "multiple reflections in multiple mirrors," in which you "see yourself going this way and you see yourself going that way."[5] The poems in *Myths & Texts* and in sections of *Mountains and Rivers Without End* touch on the most basic, deeply felt mythological ground, and they do what myth has always done: they give us some access to the intense instance of our lives in the vast series of interrelationships established by the figures, events, and images of the myth.

All of Gary Snyder's study and work has been directed toward a poetry that would approach phenomena with a disciplined clarity and that would then use the "archaic" and "primitive" as models to once again see this poetry as woven through all parts of our lives. Thus it draws its substance and forms from the broadest range of a people's day-to-day lives, enmeshed in the facts of work, the real trembling in joy and grief, thankfulness for good crops, the health of a child, the warmth of the lover's touch. Further, Snyder seeks to recover a poetry that could sing and thus relate us to: magpie, beaver, a mountain range, binding us to all these other lives, seeing our spiritual lives as bound up in the rounds of nature.

Snyder's concerns are, as Luis Ellicott Yglesias recently noted, "archaic in the primal sense—a going into the deep past not to escape or to weep with loud lamentations, but to see whether with the help of the earth-lore that is 'all forgot' it might be possible to open life to a more livable future."[6] In terms of any future we may have, Snyder's look toward the primitive may vouchsafe one of the only real alternative directions available. The world view of primitive man, close to the "world, in its nakedness, which is fundamental for all of us— birth, love, death; the sheer fact of being alive" (*Earth House Hold,* 118), engenders, in its attention to the round of birth and death, great carefulness and reverence toward life. That care and reverence are lost when the awareness of these relationships is shattered. Apart from its many rich bequests, one of Western civilization's legacies is a destructive alienation from the "ground of its own being," (*Turtle Island,* 106), a denial of biological reality. And as Terrence Des Pres noted in *The Survivor,* this refusal and "the denial of death come finally to be a denial of life. . . . There is terrible irony in this, for whereas awareness of death generates firm care for life, death-denial ends in a fury of destruction. Amid high cant and pieties obscenely cynical, whole cities and peoples are wiped out."[7]

The anthropologist Stanley Diamond has stated that the "sickness of civilization consists . . . in its failure to incorporate (and only then) to move beyond the limits of the primitive."[8] Taking up the oldest songs, extending them and sustaining them, is a part then of what Gary Snyder has called "the real work of modern man: to uncover the inner structure and actual boundaries of the mind" (*Earth House Hold,* 127).

What then of the interviews and talks collected here in the context of Snyder's poetry? A lot of what follows is simply good, plain talk with a man who has a lively and very subtle mind and a wide range of experience and knowledge. But there is one important aspect of these texts that I'd like to follow out for a moment: the place of the interview in our literature.

Scholars today take for granted the journals, workbooks and letters of authors as important source materials. And though primarily personal, these different kinds of writing have led in significant directions beyond their original bounds. Some have become recognized separate genres; such was the case with Bashō's travel diaries. Letters have provided possibilities for greatly expanding the scope of the novel in the European context. It was the introduction of the epistolary element in eighteenth-century English and German works that brought attention to the individual's inner life, a quality we now perceive to be a central element of the novel. And more recently the journal has had an increasingly important place in the work of many poets, Paul Blackburn and Allen Ginsberg among them.

The interview belongs in this continuum and it has opened a substantial range of possibilities for far-reaching discourse. In collecting a series of his own interviews, the poet Donald Hall noted that since World War II the interview had become "the dominant form by which poets made public their poetics."[9] For Gary Snyder the interview has been much more—although, indeed, some of his most incisive statements on poetics are contained in the interviews that follow. For Snyder the interview has become an occasion to publicly tie together a complex series of interests and concerns and, within the context of the dialogue generated, follow new directions suggested.

We have had the interview, in the broadest possible sense, as an established part of Western European literary tradition at least since Boswell's *Life of Johnson*. By the end of the eighteenth century, the practice of recording notable statements of important poets and writers had intensified—a development well exemplified in Eckermann's *Conversations with Goethe* and Coleridge's *Table Talk*.

The rise of the literary interview has been dependent upon a concern with the individual writer's particular state of mind, a concern that marks the beginnings of modern literature. But if the interview benefits us in the attention it brings to an individual writer's practice, it also shares in the excesses of an extreme and quirky individualism. Interviews with writers often circle constantly about the individual writer's personal life. Wendell Berry has recently criticized the literary interview precisely because of these kinds of concerns. He notes in many interviews a tendency to hold in high regard the "personal circumstances, and casual opinions of poets" and finds alarming the fact that the motivating idea often seems to be "to *examine* the poet, to study as unobtrusively as possible whatever privacies may be disclosed by the inadvertencies of conversation."[10] We can add to that the gossip inherent in random talk, the slight tendency detected by Jerome Rothenberg for poets to "begin lying in the process" of the interview, and the overblown quality often lent to even the slightest offhand remark.[11]

But these are almost necessary historical features of the literary interview, and they will play themselves out. I think there is a turn away from this overt personal concern, and that it can be seen in those dialogues where the poetic intelligence is led to make a series of genuinely new connections generated in the talking. The current popularity of the interview reflects, on its most intense level, an exploratory quality in modern American poetic theory and practice, what George Quasha has called the "dialogical" in modern poetics.[12] In those instances where the interview is generated by this kind of participation, it not only provides an open area for critical discussion, it participates directly in a poetics of process, a poetry engaged, seeking to draw the listener/reader into the act of *poesis,* the active process of speaking and following out the discovery, transformation, and invention that poetry seeks.

Gary Snyder's interviews and talks belong to this line of exploratory dialogue. A part of the reason for the intensity generated in many of the interviews may lie in the fact that they have often been given in the context of readings. Poets are repeatedly asked for interviews as they travel around the country, and such exchanges are thus often another manifestation of the natural dialogue that arises around the margins of poetry readings.

One final note then on a tradition that relates directly to the substance of this book. The question-and-answer (Japanese: *mondo*) and the recorded saying (Japanese: *goroku*) are Buddhist texts of what were originally orally transmitted teachings, talks given on a specific occasion or addressing a certain question, spoken freely, spontaneously. The teachings of these texts (the *Lin-chi-Lu* or *Record of Rinzai* is perhaps the single most important text for Snyder) inform Snyder's talk, but more than the content material of these texts it is perhaps the direction the dialogue often takes—turning the question back around to the one who asked—that bears on the interviews that follow. There is a web of interests and concerns that remains constant in these talks, but rather than viewing the texts as representing any final statement on those issues, I think Gary Snyder would like to see the process that initiated the questioning sustained, bringing many of the questions raised back to the individual reader's own life.

Scott McLean
August 1979
Nevada County, California

NOTES

[1] Henry David Thoreau, *Writings* (Boston and New York: Houghton Mifflin Co., 1906), VI, 160. See also, Novalis, *Werke,* ed. Gerhard Schulz (München: C. H. Beck, 1969), pp. 278, 326.

[2] William Carlos Williams, *Imaginations* (New York: New Directions, 1970), p. 102.

[3] Statement by Snyder at the Berkeley Poetry Conference, 1965.

[4] Donald Wesling, "Thoroughly Modern Measures," *Boundary 2,* 3 (1975), 460.

[5] Gary Snyder, "Interview," in *Towards a New American Poetics,* ed. Ekbert Faas (Santa Barbara: Black Sparrow Press, 1978), p. 135.

[6] Luis Ellicott Yglesias, "Fear and Trembling in New Hampshire," *New Boston Review,* June/July 1979, p. 26.

[7] Terrence Des Pres, *The Survivor* (New York: Oxford University Press, 1976), pp. 206, 207.

[8] Stanley Diamond, *In Search of the Primitive* (New Brunswick, N.J.: Transaction Books, 1974), p. 129.

[9] Donald Hall, *Goatfoot Milktongue Twinbird* (Ann Arbor: University of Michigan Press, 1978), p. ix.

[10] Wendell Berry, "The Specialization of Poetry," *Hudson Review,* 28 (1975), 11, 14.

[11] Jerome Rothenberg, "Craft Interview," in *The Craft of Poetry,* ed. William Packard (Garden City, N.Y.: Doubleday, 1974), p. 37.

[12] See his "DiaLogos: Between the Written and the Oral in Contemporary Poetry," *New Literary History,* 8 (1977), 485–506.

THE REAL WORK

THE LANDSCAPE OF CONSCIOUSNESS

Gene Fowler conducted the following interview in December of 1964, and it was published that year in the Literary Times *(Chicago). Fowler was Snyder's student during the academic year 1964–65, when the latter taught at the University of California, Berkeley. They rode together across the Bay Bridge from Berkeley to San Francisco on Snyder's motorcycle; the interview was held in Snyder's apartment on Green Street in North Beach.*

FOWLER: You have written that as a poet you "hold the most archaic values on earth . . . the fertility of the soil, the magic of animals, the power-vision in solitude, the terrifying initiation and rebirth, the love and ecstasy of the dance, the common work of the tribe." Do these values enter, pretty much at a conscious level, into your selection of subjects to treat and poetic tools to use or reject?

SNYDER: Not really at a conscious or deliberate level, I think. These values are very basic to me, and to my friends. They're, in the Buddhist sense, rooted in the belly; and this is where the breath starts, so where the poem starts. I think these concerns are basic to everyone, but most don't think about them, aren't aware of them. They buy vegetables in the supermarket, but don't think about the soil these grow in; they keep pets, but don't look into an animal's eyes and see an intelligence there, a sensibility; they are driven into solitude, into their own personality, by the stresses of our culture, but don't look for new strength there. At that point "initiation and rebirth" is possible outside a religious structure. Everybody wants to know the ecstasy of the dance.

As for the common work of the tribe: most think they're working for themselves; but that just isn't how it is. My poems, on one level, call the society's attention to its ecological relationships in nature, and to its relationships in the individual consciousness. Some of the poems show how society doesn't see its position in nature. What are we going to do with this planet? It's a problem of love; not the humanistic love of the West—but a love that extends to animals, rocks, dirt, all of it. Without this love, we can end, even without war, with an uninhabitable place.

FOWLER: Could you say something more about the power-vision in solitude?

SNYDER: The power-vision is not concerned with political power, but the knowledge of the self, the power of no-power; this is in the practice of Zen. But it's not limited to Zen; it's a basic human possibility that can be uncovered any place, any time. It's, in part, a process of tearing yourself out of your personality and your culture and putting yourself back in it again. When we can gear in at this point, where the roles we all enact—old man, wise child, virgin, hag, et cetera—and the most personal perceptions come together, we can see ourselves as "social man." We can reach beyond our social nature and see our relationships in nature, or reach inward and see the relationships that hold there. It's here, too, that we can understand the Buddhist concept of oneness and uniqueness: our social or ritual nature and our personal perception. It's at this level of awareness that I feel all these relationships; my best poems come from such a state and plot these relationships for a listener, who really knew about them but didn't know he knew.

FOWLER: After a good many years of making poems, do you have some ideas about what makes a poem go sour or fail to go off?

SNYDER: I don't think I can answer that about my poems. The thing that keeps someone else's poem from working for me most often is too much ego interference, too much abstract intellect, too much striving for effect; there's a lack of contact with the inner voices.

FOWLER: Some time back you said your poems were exploring job and place; recently you said your poems were now exploring the architecture of consciousness. Why do you think the nature of your explorations changed? What are some of the ways in which you explore this architecture in the poems, or through the act of making a poem?

SNYDER: I think the change in emphasis just happened over a period of time. Some of the openings that occurred as a result of Zen disciplines are involved; but I can't say just how. In the statement you refer to, I almost used "landscape" rather than "architecture." This goes back to the landscape nature of the values we covered at the beginning. More and more I am aware of very close correspondences between the external and internal landscape. In my long poem, *Mountains and Rivers Without End,* I'm dealing with these correspondences, moving back and forth. We see this in the rituals of children's games, in the psychological techniques of shamans. By "architecture of consciousness" I mean the structure of the whole mind, from contentless ground through the unconscious and conscious, and on out through sense perception and immediate emotion into the reaches of abstract, scientific theorizing and pure mathematics. My poems, I think, show a few of these relationships and we can get a closer look at the range of it all. As Duncan says, we often bring up awarenesses we didn't know about. It's at this point the poem becomes an exploration, an adventure.

I'd emphasize again the importance of a sense of community, a need for the poet to identify with *real* people, not a faceless audience. There should be less concern with publishing, more with reading. A reading is a kind of communion. I think the poet articulates the semi-known for the tribe. This is close to the ancient function of the shaman.[1]* It's not a dead function. The poet needs a long view. He can't just plan in terms of a few poems to be done immediately. He may be

* Footnote numbers in the body of the text refer to the section "Some Further Angles," beginning p. 175.

5

eighty years old before he's ready to do his masterwork. The creative imagination doesn't stop growing like the body. It keeps growing and getting ready to strike deeper into the basic relationships between the personal perception, the social ritual movements, and nature. Poetry is a life's work.

THE *BERKELEY BARB* INTERVIEW

One side of the Japanese national character has influenced Gary Snyder's poetry considerably: the people's attention in their daily work to the immediate task at hand. This attentiveness, reflected especially in the section, "Far East," of The Back Country, *brought to Snyder's poetry an acute awareness of subject/object interrelationships. But it is not an element unique to the poetry written during and after Snyder's years in Japan; this careful attention to the immediate represents rather the intensification of an attitude of mind already present in the early poetry collected in* Riprap *(1959). In an interview not collected here (Ananke, 1965), Snyder touched on his own poetic practice and development with specific reference to his poems from Japan and to daily activities "pervaded by mindfulness":*

> *One of my poems* ["February," *in* The Back Country] *is about doing a lot of little chores around the house. It is very close to what I am thinking of, in a very obvious way, of the act and the thought being together. And, in that sense, there is a body-mind dualism if I am sweeping the floor and thinking about Hegel. But if I am sweeping the floor and thinking about sweeping the floor, I am all one. And that is not trivial, nor is the sensation of it trivial. Sweeping the floor becomes, then, the most important thing in the world. Which it is.*

*   *   *

> *My first start in this direction was at the same time I began writing all the poems I consider worthwhile. That was when I*

was working for a trail crew up in Yosemite Park. I found myself doing three months of long, hard physical labor, out on the trails every day, living more or less in isolation, twenty-five miles from the nearest road. We never went out. We just stayed in there working on those trails week after week. At the beginning, I found myself straining against it, trying to exercise my mind as I usually exercise it. I was reading Milton, and I had some other reading, and I was trying to go out on the trails during the day and think about things in a serious, intellectual way, while doing my work. And it was frustrating, although I had done the same thing before, on many jobs. Finally, I gave up trying to carry on an intellectual interior life separate from the work, and I said the hell with it, I'll just work. And instead of losing something, I got something much greater. By just working, I found myself being completely there, having the whole mountain inside of me, and finally having a whole language inside of me that became one with the rocks and with the trees. And that was where I first learned the possibility of being one with what you were doing, and not losing anything of the mind thereby.

The following interview, given immediately after Snyder's return to California in late 1968, gives yet another angle on Snyder's years in Japan. It treats his views of Japanese countercultural movements in the late sixties and his involvement with the wandering poet Nanao Sakaki.

The interviewer is Keith Lampe, an old friend whom Snyder had first met in Japan. In 1968 Lampe was a writer for the Berkeley Barb, *where the interview first appeared (January 1969).*

LAMPE: What sort of interesting things were happening in Japan when you left?

SNYDER: Well, the gradual emergence of what we call a subculture—the beginnings of the emergence—were visible in Japan in the last couple of years. And this is much newer for Japan than it is for the West.

LAMPE: What forms specifically was it taking?

SNYDER: In the last three or four years the numbers of interested young people have grown to the point that now the particular circle that I'm thinking of has a group community on an island, another community farm in the mountains, and a community house in Tokyo—and all three of these centers are open to all the members of this group, the members not being narrowly defined in any way and all of them moving freely, hitchhiking, from place to place among all these three. Each one of them having some particular kind of work to do which contributes to the economic welfare of the whole.

LAMPE: So the people are able to act out a kind of full circle, or cycle—mountain, farm, and city?

SNYDER: Well, it's mountain farm, island farm, and city. Those are the three. And they always are stimulating. And they have plans for extending into other areas of Japan, other localities.

At the moment, they have one center in Tokyo. They have another center on one of the southernmost islands of Japan—a tiny island at the subtropical southern borders of the country where banana trees grow. They have another one in the mountains at about 3,000–4,000 feet elevation—not so far from Tokyo, an area that has lots of snow in the winter and chestnut trees and ice-skating and wintery crops to grow—and they're next projecting getting some land up in the northernmost island of Hokkaido, which has a Siberian ecology and echoes of the Ainu culture and of the Siberian Gilyak culture from prehistoric times.

And they like to think of themselves as gradually embracing all of the ancient marginal possibilities of Japanese culture—like the Okinawan Malayo-Polynesian southern branch and also finally the Gilyak proto-American Indian northern branch. The name that they give themselves in Japanese is *buzoku,* which means tribe, simply. They call themselves the tribe.

I think maybe they got that word partly from what they'd heard of what was going on in the United States and in Europe, but they mean it very much in their own way. Tribe.

9

They have a very clear sense of what tribal social organization implies as an alternative to the kind of social organization we find in class-structured civilized modern states.

By "modern" I mean the last two thousand years. The idea of "nation" or "country" is so solidly established in most people's consciousness now that there's no intelligent questioning of it. It's taken for granted as some kind of a necessity. The sense of tribal social structure is one of the ways of breaking out of that nation-state bag, another way of seeing how large groups of people can relate to and organize each other without having a "social contract."

Part of our failure in understanding Africa, Southeast Asia—and India, for that matter—is our inability to deal with groups of people who see themselves tribally rather than in terms of a nation.

LAMPE: Do you think the younger people in Japan will be able to establish a really independent subculture faster than we can here in the States?

SNYDER: Maybe they can because nobody's paying any attention to them. The Japanese people as a whole are not particularly interested. They don't have this sick fascination with it, nor do they have any particular hostility to it. They don't see it as a danger—although it is. And the Japanese subculture is not hung up on getting publicity, nor, given their particular social situation, are they feeling that they have to accomplish everything this year. So that they're willing to dig in and work longer.

Within that context they also have working in their favor the gradual breakdown of "progress" and the problems that are bound to come with heavy industrialization . . . and with the breakup of the traditional Japanese social order. They're way ahead of it all. They're farther ahead of things than anybody else in Japan. They see what the future holds in terms of industry and where science and the implications of science *can* lead and at the same time they have an excellent grasp on the archaic origins of Japanese culture.

If you have a grasp on the future and on your historical roots

10

simultaneously, you can't lose. And they've got that. Ordinary Japanese people have a limited grasp. For them Japanese tradition means the last three or four hundred years and for them science and scientific programs mean the nineteenth and twentieth centuries. If you can think about what the Neolithic was and what the twenty-second century will be, simultaneously, then you've got it. I think that's true for here, too.

Japanese society is much tougher than American society. If you drop out for a couple of years after graduating from college and wander around leading a semibohemian way of life, you can't get back into that society and have a job. Let alone, say, drop out in high school and take up hitchhiking around and living on the streets.

The "tribe" people have lived so much closer to the economic bottom than anybody in this country ever knows that in some ways there's no comparison. Now what they have is the real strength of hitting the bottom and surviving.

What they have all done is each one of them separately hit the bottom and survived and then discovered there were some others who had hit the bottom. And from that they have formed a little subculture of their own.

The thing that is most interesting about them, to me, in terms of comparison with the American subculture, is that they don't have any backing from the society, from parents, from welfare, from anywhere. They have really cut themselves off. Nobody's going to give them a dime. What you often hear about hippies in this country, they're getting supported by their middle-class parents, is all too true a lot of the time.

Now here's a group of people who have literally dropped out so thoroughly that they have to learn how to make it together. Because they have to learn how to make it together, they don't cheat each other. They're reliable with each other.

It's because of this real level of necessity and total commitment to this role that they have a kind of strength and courage and a kind of group unity that is very exciting to see.

And they have hit their own level of independence and individual freedom, which is rare in Japan because it's not a society which creates individuals or individualism. And then they've been able, on top of their individualism, their sense of individual personal destiny, to add a discipline of cooperation and living and working together.

Their leader or leading teacher is a man named Nanao Sakaki. Sakaki was in the air force in World War Two. He's in his forties now. His experience in the air force turned him over so much that after the war was over he never went back home. First he went up to Tokyo and he lived under the bridges with the beggars and the prostitutes for a few years. Then he took to walking and begging his way all over Japan— and he walked the total length of Japan several times over.

During that period, stopping in public libraries and school-teachers' houses in the country and so forth, he taught himself to read English and Greek—and later he taught himself to read Sanskrit. And he educated himself in anthropology and biology and astronomy and history while walking Japan back and forth from one end to the other.

After ten years or fifteen years of this kind of living, he gradually began to know some young dropout students in the Tokyo area—and at first they used to come to him where he used to hang out on some river banks on the outskirts of Tokyo making junk sculpture. They would come and talk to him and they would say, "What would be interesting for us to do?" And he would say, "Go to the northern end of Hokkaido and come back—and don't have more than a hundred yen on you when you start. And then I'll talk to you."

He would set them to these little projects, like going a thousand miles with no money, and if they came back, then he would start talking to them. And he would advise them to read. And what he would advise them to read would be Herodotus and the ancient Chinese historian Ssu-ma Chien. . . .

His style still sets the style in that he's the one who can always say, "Don't ever tell me you need anything." And the less we've got the happier we should be for it—and the more grateful we should be. (*Laughs.*) And the worse that happens to us, the more grateful we are because it reminds us that we don't need anything. Everything starts from nothing and we have the power of that behind us.

Nanao got the word that one of the southern islands off Kyushu was underpopulated because it was too isolated and the soil was too bad and that no one would object if some people moved in there and did some kind of homesteading.

So he and seven or eight people went down and spent the first summer doing nothing but cutting back the bamboo, tearing out the roots and planting sweet potatoes. The second summer was last summer. I was with them both summers for part of the time. I don't mean to say that they do this just in the summer. They've been doing this continually since they started, but the summer's been the biggest push in land-clearing.

Last summer we cleared some more land, burned the brush, burned the stumps, rooted out more land, put more into cultivation, and simultaneously we were able to cut lumber and drag it down from the hills and square off logs toward building a house.

During that period, because of typhoon weather, the ship didn't come. The ship only comes once a week and this little ship can't even come into the island. It has to stop offshore and then a boat goes out to it.

Because the ship didn't come, the food ran out. And this is a common thing for that ashram: to be out of food for three weeks or four weeks at a time. As we ran short on rations, we simply cut down the daily amount of food for everybody to two meals a day—a bowl and a half of gruel per person at a meal—and scrounged up on the countryside, got edible nuts. Because of the heavy surf we weren't able to do much fishing but we were able to gather shellfish. And we tried out some additional wild plants that we hadn't tried before.

LAMPE: How many people are into this level of things?

SNYDER: There are always ten to twenty in the island ashram, there are always twenty to thirty probably up in the Fujimi Mountain ashram, there are always thirty or forty people living in the central commune in Tokyo and there are probably two or three hundred people that are circulating . . .

They also work on the docks; they work on railroad construction and repair; they pick up odd jobs anywhere they are in the country, and they drift in and they drift out. And they have a real sense of sharing—so that you give somebody a sweater and over the next year you see the same sweater on ten or fifteen different people because they just keep passing it along.

LAMPE: Where do you plan to live now that you're back in the States?

SNYDER: Somewhere in the country. The country is the revolutionary territory. I'm not saying it's the only one, but for me it's the ground to live and work in. I want to get out there and agitate them trees and grasses into revolting against the exploiting class . . . (*laughing*) . . . stir up a few earthquakes and volcanic eruptions.

ROAD APPLE INTERVIEW WITH GARY SNYDER

The interview with Doug Flaherty first appeared in Road Apple *(1969/70), a small magazine that Flaherty edited, published in Oshkosh, Wisconsin.*

FLAHERTY: When you began writing poetry, what was it that made you turn to Oriental philosophy instead of sticking to the American Indian legends of your own environment?

SNYDER: For one thing I don't think that I understood the richness and complexity of traditional primitive cultures. For another thing, traditional Hinduism and Buddhism have added a great deal onto basic shamanistic and primitive ritualistic ceremonial practices and life styles.[2] That is a great value. There is nothing in primitive cultures that is at all equivalent to Mahayana philosophy or logic. There is a science and true sophistication of certain states of mind and power that can come through shamanism but the shaman himself doesn't understand the power. Buddhism and yoga have been gradually evolving as a true science of the mind and science of the nature of things but of a different order from the physical sciences we've had so far, called in Sanskrit *Shri Vidya,* or the holy science.

The Buddhist and Hindu traditions, although they specialized in and progressed greatly in the realms of philosophy, yoga, and extraordinary meditative techniques, also lost something

15

which the primitives did have, and that was a total integrated life style. They were able to develop within civilization to a high degree, but they lost their community relations and their ability to have a family and they had to become celibate in the monastic tradition. Certain primitive cultures that are functioning on a high level actually amount to what would be considered a spiritual training path in which everyone in the culture is involved and there are no separations between the priest and layman or between the men who become enlightened and those who can't. What we need to do now is to take the great intellectual achievement of the Mahayana Buddhists and bring it back to a community style of life which is not necessarily monastic. Some Native American groups are a good example.

FLAHERTY: Could you explain a bit further the example that the Indian style of life offers us?

SNYDER: Teaching should begin with what the local forces are. You can learn a great deal of ecology and geology from your area. But to give another dimension to that, you have to consult the Indian mythology and ritual and magic of the area and try to understand why it was they saw certain figures as potent. Why do the Winnebago see the hare as potent? Also, economic use of the land by Indians is very illuminating. If you want to know what it is you would do if you were taken back to rock bottom, and what you would have to do to survive in your region, then you would have to consult the first people. What did they eat? What did they make fibers of? What did they make soap out of? What did they use for medicine? What were their basic materials—economic botany in other words. They painted their bodies red? Where did they get their pigments? All of these things are right under your feet.

And even though you might never have to use them in any economic sense, it is a great extension of one's awareness of place. You should really know what the complete natural world of your region is and know what all its interactions are and how you are interacting with it yourself. This is just part of the work of becoming who you are, where you are. There are also certain kinds of intellectual studies and psychological and spiritual practices which are more universal, which have a broader reference than any given locality. And even those can benefit from some reference to the people of Place. Some of the Buddhist symbols we use are kind of arbitrary and some of these symbols could just as well be translated into terms of the North American continent.

FLAHERTY: What is the quality that you find in the Orient that can't be found here?

SNYDER: The Orient has a more enormous teaching tradition intact. There are several great wisdom traditions with teachers and schools. They also have them in North America, but unless you are born as a member of a certain Pueblo and have the right to enter a certain kiva, you can't get into these schools. They have some little odds and ends of schools like these within Christianity but again they are very difficult to approach, and their symbolism and language is perhaps not as available to us really as the language, the terminology of Sanskrit and Chinese Buddhism. . . .

FLAHERTY: In Zen, they speak of satori. How does this influence your poetry?

SNYDER: I don't lay claim to any great enlightenment experiences or anything like that, but I have had a very moving, profound perception a few times that everything was alive (the basic perception of animism) and that on one level there is no hierarchy of qualities in life—that the life of a stone or a weed is as completely beautiful and authentic, wise and valuable as the life of, say, an Einstein. And that Einstein and the weed know this; hence the preciousness of mice and weeds.

FLAHERTY: How does the state or condition of *meditation* fit into your notion of the authenticity of experience?

SNYDER: There's nothing exotic about meditation. It's a birthright of everybody. Animals know all about it. Animals have the capacity for sitting still and tuning in on their own inside consciousness, as well as the outside consciousness, for great periods of time. And they can restore themselves by doing that; you can see them doing it. The calmness of deer at rest at midday is the order of meditation. It's a curious thing that Western

17

man has gotten so anxious about it and has forgotten what it is and really looks askance on anyone doing it. Most of the rest of the world knows how to meditate and does so in one way or another.

It's a great oversight not to take the time to look at what your mind is doing and what your body is really like and what speech is when something rises from within, that makes you want to utter a sound. So meditation is sitting still and cutting off the inputs and the distractions and the things that are always leading you from one thing to the next thing to the next—just stopping that stream of often very trivial and inattentive acts and creating a condition of attention in which you look within and try to see what the mind is doing on its own within you—a completely natural thing to do.

FLAHERTY: In some forms of Oriental studies, the subject attempts to reach the *void*. You're not thinking of placing everything outside of mind. You're speaking of thinking things out, aren't you?

SNYDER: Meditation is a very broad term which includes a number of different interior exercises that can be done once put in a position of no inputs. The condition of no inputs is best achieved by sitting in the half-lotus or the full-lotus with your back straight in a quiet place and breathing in a certain way from the diaphragm. So posture is important. Then, if you're working as a Buddhist, according to the tradition that you are studying, your meditative exercises may proceed in several possible directions although ultimately they will all complete the different areas that they are exploring. One may start out exploring a certain way but they will all come back to the complete view of the whole eventually, which is a trip to the ground of being, below and more fundamental than any kind of mental content, any symbols or any archetypes or visions.

FLAHERTY: To turn to the poet, do you find that the poem is the ultimate end of this type of meditation?

SNYDER: Poetry comes into this at many levels. Poetry *is* before it *begins* in a sense. Like stopping a person momentarily in their tracks with a poem they have happened to look at accidentally and they forget that they were to catch a bus some-where and they look around and think: My God, I'm living in the world! Or like the great enlightened poet saints like Milarepa or Zen Buddhist masters who wrote poetry. They wrote poetry at the height of their delight, the sheer play of being. Or they would trade poems with each other that other people had written. So the poem always stands there as almost the essence of it. And the beauty of it is that at the beginning and at the end it is equal. That the poem is as valid for the Zen master who is seeing through it, as it is for the man on the street who suddenly remembers that it is spring because the poem has turned his head from his preoccupation. That's one way of looking at it. Another way is to simply see it as classes of poems that work in different ways. That's historically true. There are work poems, love poems, war poems, or actually songs. And there are en-lightenment songs and there are healing songs. In a sense poetry is really the dance at the top of the whole process because it's going out into emptiness and into the formless which is the na-ture of pure joy. And what do you do then? You sing. Look at Milarepa. The songs are almost a folk narrative which is on the order of legend or myth. They are accounts of Milarepa going here, Milarepa going there, and having to fight the genial de-mons and converting them all to Buddhism. Really beautiful and profound, and close to the people.

Another type of poetry is the great Chinese poetry of the T'ang Dynasty which, for a century or two, was for some strange reason on a very high level. They weren't Zen monks or anything although they were all of the same milieu. The great Chinese poets were contemporaries of all the great Chi-nese masters even though they might not have known each other very much because China had a huge population even then. It's a real cultural high point; poetry and Zen were both at their most creative in China simultaneously.

FLAHERTY: And what about your own poetry? It seems in-sufficient to call it "neoromantic" or back to nature. How could we describe it?

SNYDER: I see my poetry as falling into two classes. I write lyrical poems which are shorter and which are pretty easy to understand on one level. I like to write poems that have at least one level that people can get into right away such as those in *Riprap* and *The Back Country*. The other type is that which I did in *Myths and Texts* and which I am doing in *Mountains and Rivers Without End* which is more on the order of working with myths and symbols and ideas. Working with old traditions and insights. What would you call them?

FLAHERTY: Would you call them *elemental* poems?

SNYDER: No, not really precise enough for me. Everything is elemental.

FLAHERTY: Well, I use the term elemental to apply to specific, universal natural conditions. I was thinking of your poetry as dealing with an elemental relationship between man and his environment as opposed to many American poets who are all hung up on middle-class social subjects.

SNYDER: Well, I look at most of my stuff as being on a myth-making order as opposed to a lyric order. Or a ritual and magic order as against a pure song order.

FLAHERTY: You mentioned before that you don't use nature or animal symbols in your poetry unless you have actually seen them. Could you develop this idea which is basically, I suppose, a realistic approach to poetry as opposed to the old notion of the use of imagination?

SNYDER: I apply that principle automatically. Maybe it is unimaginative of me, but if I don't have a ground of actual physical experience I don't make reference to it, if I can help it, in almost any area. I don't invent things out of my head unless it is an actual experience—like seeing a bear in a dream, this is a true mode of seeing a bear.

FLAHERTY: This type of "experience in the head"—is this in some way for you tied in with the teachings of the *Bhagavad-Gita*?

SNYDER: I might be misunderstanding the *Gita* in some ways, but there is a tendency in Hinduism to go out there to a mind-breaking absolute point of seeing only that side of all things being impermanent, all things being illusory, and all things ultimately returning into Shiva, or the all-devouring mouth of Krishna, which can be an excuse for having no responsibility to anything on your own plane. The Mahayana Buddhists think one step beyond that, that is to say, beyond the ultimate void is *this*.

FLAHERTY: By *this* you mean everything created?

SNYDER: Yes. And because the universe is empty, and infinite, and eternal. Because of that, weeds are precious, mice are precious. And the other heart of Buddhist experience is something that can't be talked about. Sometimes it can be hinted at or approached in some poems.

FLAHERTY: Do you mean that this "experience" is knowledge of the world that cannot be put into words? Or that it cannot be reached?

SNYDER: No, it's not that it can't be reached. Simply that you can't talk about it. It's an inner order of experience that is not available to language. Language has no words to talk about it. When you put it into words you lose it; so it's better not to talk about it.

FLAHERTY: Then how does the poem fit this "order of experience"?

SNYDER: The true poem is walking that edge between what can be said and that which cannot be said. That's the real razor's edge. The poem that falls all the way over into what can be said can still be very exciting, but the farther it is from the razor's edge the less it has of the real magic. It can be very well done but the ones that make your hair stand on edge are the ones that are right on the line. And then some of them fall too much in the realm of what can't be said.

Then they are no longer poems; they are meditation themes like the koan, or they are magical incantations, or they are mantras. Mantras or koans or spells are actually superelliptical poems that the reader cannot understand except that he has to put hundreds of more hours of meditation in toward getting it than he has to put in to get the message out of a normal poem.

And the experience is correspondingly more profound than a reader usually experiences with a poem. But then it is the property of a very special practice.

Haiku has something of this quality. The haiku of Bashō and his immediate disciples have the quality of the poem pushed as far as one can push it. "The words stop but the meaning goes on."

ON EARTH GEOGRAPHY

The interview with Richard Grossinger appeared in IO, *No. 12 (1971), the first of Grossinger's Earth Geography Booklets; David Wilk, editor of* Truck, *helped Grossinger with the interview.*

It was a particularly useful encounter for it brought to the Booklets at their beginning an example of careful, detailed, direct knowledge of one particular region. In responding to Wilk's later request for suggestions on a Biogeography Workbook (Truck *18, 1978), Snyder again emphasized the need for these "fundamentals":*

> *"Biogeography" is already on the way to being a fad, with its new terms. Fundamentals are: it relates to knowing land directly, not just intellectually, with one's body, commitment, time, labor, walking. Maps, charts, botanic lists, histories, are all just the menu. You'd starve on that. Also: biogeography is political. It destroys the national state's pretensions. It cuts off exploitation. It discourages senseless travel-for-sensation. It puts libraries out of business. It knows the exact language to answer Earl Butz. It is businesslike and playful. It can nurture; it knows when to kill.*

Richard Grossinger has for many years edited North Atlantic Books and IO, *a journal whose concerns are "myth, geography, and the common source material of poetry, natural history, and physical science."*

GROSSINGER: I'll ask a general question to begin with. About regions. What sort of things you've done in your own region. Or thoughts about regionalism in general.

SNYDER: Well, the first thing is establishing the criteria for defining a region, a set of criteria, and that in itself is very interesting . . . since, even though we know better, we are accustomed to accepting the political boundaries of counties and states, and then national boundaries, as being some kind of regional definition; and although, in some cases, there is some validity to those lines, I think in many cases, and especially in the Far West, the lines are often quite arbitrary and serve only to confuse people's sense of natural associations and relationships. So, for the state of California, which is the only area I'm capable of talking about really right now, what was most useful originally for us was to look at the maps in the *Handbook of California Indians,* which showed the distribution of the original Indian culture groups and tribes (culture areas), and then to correlate that with other maps, some of which are in Kroeber's *Cultural and Natural Areas of Native North America . . .* and just correlate the overlap between ranges of certain types of flora, between certain types of biomes, and climatological areas, and cultural areas, and get a sense of that region, and then look at more or less physical maps and study the drainages, and get a clearer sense of what drainage terms are and correlate those also. All these are exercises toward breaking our minds out of the molds of political boundaries or any kind of habituated or received notions of regional distinctions.

There's a lot of background, of course, to such an interest: like why would people arrive at a point of trying to see things in that way. Without going back over all that, because I think we know that, really, I'll just say there are two things behind it. One is political; the other is ecological. The political side of it is a long-range, a long-term feeling we've all had that political entities are not real. Simply that. A political anarchist position: that the boundaries drawn by national states and so forth don't represent any sort of real entity. But that kind of perception's been a theoretical perception, whereas what gives reality to this kind of thinking now is the realization, in terms of efficient and elegant associations of natural systems (if there's going to be a condition of harmonious growth rather than outrageous growth) that we need this kind of knowledge. People have to learn a sense of region, and what is possible within a region, rather than indefinitely assuming that a kind of promiscuous distribution of goods and long-range transportation is always going to be possible.

And that brings you back into thinking more in terms of your human scope and your human scale: what can you do in an area that you can ride a horse or walk on, and what are the things that you rely on in that case, what resources do you develop. And that gives you a very strong, concrete sense of how regions and then subregions work, and makes a study of aboriginal native people's ways of life more than just an academic exercise.

GROSSINGER: How has that worked in your region?

SNYDER: Well, in our region, which is the Nevada County west slope of the Sierra, drainage of the Yuba, white settlement was determined almost entirely by the Gold Rush, and so it has no relation to anything which is on the surface; it has relation to that which is under the surface, or was, and is of almost no value now in making any sense. Other things happened, such as, because of early logging and fire a period of grazing, ranching, was made possible, which, as it turned out, was a very short-term phase; and the grass succession was rapidly replaced by the manzanita and forest succession again, and so the tendency of that whole area is to go into forest; old farms are abandoned and are turning back into woods. Consequently, nowadays any of us who think about any gardening or farming think about it in very limited terms as something which is possible in special areas but not desirable to the region as a whole (since the region produces a great deal of life without human interference, enough life to support human beings, in small numbers, in reasonable numbers). All this is part of defining . . . California.

GROSSINGER: What clue does American Indian demography give to the present state of culture in California?

SNYDER: The Indian cultures give you a sense of what California probably in some sense *is*. There have been some profound changes in the state. The greatest single change has been the draining of the Sacramento Valley and the San Joaquin Valley, the draining of the tule swamps. You see, the great central valley of California was originally a vast area of swamp; tule is a type of reed or rush that grew in abundance in the swamps. The state has been profoundly altered, first with the Spanish grazing and ranching, and then later with the deliberate agriculture, the draining of the swamps of the great central valley. The great central valley itself was never a place of much habitation. Indians lived on the margins of it, in the eastern margins and the western margins, in zones between the hills and the valley, the hills and the plains, where they would be able to draw up higher into the hills in the winter and be above the rather chilly tule fogs, and move out into the tule swamps in the summer and other times of year when it was convenient for varieties of wild plants that were edible and out there, and for hunting the tule elk, and for snaring and netting and trapping the millions upon millions of waterfowl that pass through, and also there are large herds of pronghorn antelopes in the central valley. And the grasses of the plains and hills were different from the grasses you see now; they were all perennial bunch grasses . . . whereas the grasses now are all European grasses, mostly annuals, which has reduced the quality of the range. So that the richness of enormous swamps, plains, was drained, and the waterfowl were all shot off and it's been turned over to tractor agriculture. The tule elk is virtually extinct. The draining of swamps and the destruction of the waterfowl flocks all took place in the same period, in the 1850s and '60s, and that was a period of intense market hunting where what would now be considered game birds were sold in the marketplace, in large numbers, at dirt cheap prices, by people who went out and shot them commercially, with giant shotguns that would kill three hundred at one blast. And that's what Raymond Dasmann has described as, that single period between 1850 and 1865, the greatest single destruction of wildlife for its period of time in the history of the world . . . taking place right there in California.

GROSSINGER: You were saying something about Sauer and local agriculture.

SNYDER: Sauer says the Mediterranean is the best model for California agriculture because we have summer drought and wet winters, which is not typical of the rest of the country.

GROSSINGER: You were speaking earlier of that signature with the mushroom and the deer.

SNYDER: I was simply saying that with the rains, and the snows in the high country, the deer move down, and, as it happened this year, the rains brought the deer down, and brought the deer mushroom out at exactly the same period of time, so that the deer arrived and began to eat the deer mushroom, which was there waiting for them. They smell it under the oak duff, and they kick back the oak leaves, and find it.

GROSSINGER: Is the fact of the nation being so large and complex part of the inevitable spur toward regionalism?

SNYDER: I'm not saying that the continent as a whole, or even the planet as a whole, cannot be, in some sense, grasped and understood, and indeed it should be, but for the time, especially in North America, we are extremely deficient in regional knowledge—what's going on within a given region at any given time of year. Rather than being limiting, that gives you a lot of insight into understanding the whole thing, the larger system.

GROSSINGER: This leads me to ask you to say something again about the lost technology, the one we've lost in taking on this one.

SNYDER: There's a lost technology, and there's a ghost technology that was never developed that always existed like a ghost somewhere off to the side . . . and they are similar; they are both technologies of independence and decentralization, and decentralized energy sources. First of all, with our present technology, we tend to forget that there were a number of very workable and, in some cases, downright elegant solutions to our daily problems of life on the farm, in the eighteenth century, which was kind of the high point, that we've forgotten about, and we tend to exaggerate the problems human beings would have if . . . there were no fossil fuels simply because of our ignorance of what the other ways of doing it were, that those methods are there . . . like waterwheels. Who uses waterwheels any more to grind flour? An interesting example is the Pelton Wheel. The Pelton Wheel was developed by a mining engineer named Lester Pelton, who lived in Camptonville, California, only 25 miles from where I am, as a maximal efficiency waterwheel.

* * *

GROSSINGER: What would you say to someone who didn't want to do farm work, who, in fact, wanted to be liberated from it because it's back-breaking?

SNYDER: It's only back-breaking if you're trying to maintain a standard of living that's out of proportion to who and where you are and is dictated by the tastes of the city rather than the tastes of the country, which is what nineteenth-century American farm tastes were dictated by. That whole nineteenth-century notion forced white people into outdoing themselves while farming. And, in many cases, they had not even been in the region long enough to develop the sophistication that would have made their farming appropriate. It takes a long time to get to know how to live in a region gently and easily and with a maximal annual efficiency. That back-breaking farm work of Anglo settlers out on the Plains and in the Midwest was hard because they were ignorant and competitive, and pushed by a capitalist system from behind. They went into hock to do their farming, for tools and for seed. And a lot of them never got out of debt.

There's a whole capitalist and mercantile presence behind the frontier. An alternative to look at, if you're curious, are the Spanish-American farms, farming communities, that developed in the Upper Rio Grande Valley and the tributaries of the Rio Grande Valley, that had been there for almost three hundred years, that developed a Spanish-derived agriculture in North America on a stable basis, and although they were poor, their backs were not broken and they were never alienated or in a position of having no culture. . . . They had a strong stable Spanish-American Catholic culture, which was in relative harmony with the surrounding Indian cultures too. Then the Pueblos are a case of an agricultural stability that allows plenty of time and does not break the back. They work very hard, but they also have festivals two weeks long.

GROSSINGER: What would you say to people who say that they're isolated?

SNYDER: In relation to what? Nobody is really ever isolated. The question seems to be whether or not they're able in whatever, say, lonely region they think they're in, to have a cooperative or semicooperative community function . . . or to what degree sharing takes place with neighbors, and in that process, to what degree that circle of neighbors is able to establish a sense of its own center, its own knowledge, its own magic . . . or it remains dependent on news from outside, and thus feels continually in a cultural backwater. This is one of the strangest problems of this century . . . that business of whether or not you can feel you're at the center or whether or not you feel you're in a backwater. It's paradoxical that Portland, Maine, feels like it's a backwater, but maybe some hippie commune deeper in the hills doesn't feel like it's a backwater.

To serve mankind's interests well and to make the greatest possible development of the creative potential available does not require either numbers of human beings or a complex society. The exploration of consciousness itself and the unfolding recognition of the same principles which are at work in our own minds as being the exact principles that are operating around us is the most beautiful of possible human experiences, at least for some time to come yet, and something of that order is what is—quote—what the development of human society should serve . . . because, among other things, that teaches you that you're not alone, or that you cannot act simply for yourself . . . that teaches you that you are in an interdependent condition with other beings, and it teaches you the sanctity of life, and also how to take life; it solves, not exactly solves, but makes meaningful and beautiful the primary paradoxes that human beings *have* to live with, like "the food of Eskimos is souls" . . . how to deal with that, how to make that into real poetry.

GROSSINGER: It's those paradoxes that Lévi-Strauss calls sufficient motivation, for myth, society, and so on. There's no need to seek out superior causal elements; they're it.

SNYDER: As the American Indians, as the Pueblo assert, we are in a transition phase right now: between having lost our capacity to communicate directly, intuitively, and to understand the life force, and the return to that condition. We are doing hard practice, hard yoga on Earth for these thousands of years because of some errors we made. But our practice will win us back that skill, that capacity, that direct knowledge of the forces and energies of the universe. Those cannot be won by scientific inquiry or fancier tools; those can only be won by the most complex and sophisticated tool there is, the mind.

CRAFT INTERVIEW

The New York Quarterly *"Craft Interview" belongs to an extensive series of interviews about the art of writing conducted by the journal. It was given in 1973 in an office building labyrinth somewhere in Manhattan.*

NYQ: As most of your poems look on the printed page—they're staggered left, right, or indented or something, spaces here and there—are you after visual effect, musical effect, or both?

SNYDER: Well, I consider this very elemental. Most poets I know, most of my colleagues, who follow that open form structuring of the line on the page, do it with full intention as a scoring—as Charles Olson pointed out some years ago in his essay on projective verse.[3]

The placement of the line on the page, the horizontal white spaces and the vertical white spaces are all scoring for how it is to be read and how it is to be timed. Space means time. The marginal indentations are more an indication of voice emphasis, breath emphasis—and, as Pound might have called it, *logopoeia,* some of the dances of the ideas that are working within your syntactic structures.

NYQ: Do you have the poem pretty much complete inside you before you start to put it down to the paper, or is it that you hear this *tala* and that gets you into the poem, but then you are interacting with the paper—or do you use paper—do you use a tape recorder or something?

SNYDER: No, I write by hand when I write. But before I write I do it in my mind many times.

Almost the whole thing. The first step is the rhythmic measure, the second step is a set of preverbal visual images which move to the rhythmic measure, and the third step is embodying it in words—and I have learned as a discipline over the years to avoid writing until I have to. I don't put it on the page until it's ripe—because otherwise you simply have to revise on the page. So I let it ripen until it's fully formed and then try to speak the poem out, and as a rule it falls right into place and completes itself by itself, requiring only the smallest of minor readjustments and tunings to be just right to my mind.

NYQ: Do you keep a notebook?

SNYDER: I keep many notebooks—many notebooks and many useful files.

NYQ: With an idea of these visual images?

SNYDER: Visual, and also working phrases, working images as written out, even individual words, some of the words that I have since been working with. This is the way that I am working on *Mountains and Rivers Without End*.

NYQ: Do you think of one line of poetry, then, as the melody, another part as the accompaniment?

SNYDER: Only metaphorically. That leads into another area which is more structural, structural in regard to imagery over syntax. In that sense metaphorically there are some idea or image lines that are equivalent to the melody line, and some idea or image lines which are like a recurrent chorus or a recurrent subtheme, or repetitions that revolve in various ways, bringing different facets to light in the unfolding of the poem.

NYQ: Do you rewrite?

SNYDER: No. I tune, I make adjustments, I tamper with it just a little bit—

NYQ: So that once you have the poem down and you put your name at the end of it, that's it?

SNYDER: Well, once in a while a poem will come out half-formed, and what I'll do with that is put it aside totally for several months and then refer back to it again and then revisualize it all. I'll replay the whole experience again in my mind. I'll forget all about what's on the page and get in contact with the preverbal level behind it, and then by an effort of reexperiencing, recall, visualization, revisualization, I'll live through the whole thing again and try to see it more clearly.

NYQ: Well, this is a kind of information retrieval, almost— you were talking about notebooks and files before, and this is almost an index type of question— Do you keep those in some sort of order, or do you have cross-references?

SNYDER: Yes, they're all organized, but their only function is as mnemonic aids, like signals to open up the inner world. The inner world is too large to ever put down; it's a sea, it's an ocean; and guides and notes and things like that just help me— they're like trail-markers. It's like finding your way back to the beginning of the right path that you were on before, then you can go into it again.

NYQ: Can we talk a minute about the way you go into it— do you use meditation as a way to get into it? Is meditation a way of . . .

SNYDER: Curiously, I don't *"use"* meditation in this way, but it serves me well. I'm a practicing Buddhist, or Buddhist-shamanist, perhaps; and every day I meditate. I do zazen as a daily practice. Which does not mean that my daily meditations are poetic or necessarily profound, but I do them, and in actual fact the inception of the poem generally seems to take its beginnings more while working, rather than while sitting. But the exercise, the practice, of sitting gives me unquestionably an ease of access to the territories of my mind—and a capacity for reexperience—for recalling and revisualizing things with almost living accuracy; and I attribute that to a lot of practice of meditation; although, strictly speaking, that is not the best use of meditation.

NYQ: There's a book around called *Zen in the Art of Archery* by Eugen Herrigel which says that through a kind of disciplined inattention the archer and the target become one. The artist and the creation become one. Do you find that meditation has worked this way for you?

SNYDER: Well, yes, because, like I say, I never try to use meditation deliberately—for the reason that, as anyone who has done much meditation knows, what you aim at is never what you hit. What you consciously aim at is never what you get. Your conscious mind can't do it for you. So you do have to practice a kind of detached and careful but really relaxed in-attention, which lets the unconscious do its own thing of rising and manifesting itself. But the moment you reach out—it's like peripheral vision, almost—the moment you reach out to grab it, it slips back. It's like hunting—it's like still hunting.

Still hunting is when you take a stand in the brush or some place and then become motionless, and then things begin to become alive, and pretty soon you begin to see the squirrels and sparrows and raccoons and rabbits that were there all the time but just, you know, duck out of the way when you look at them too closely. Meditation is like that. You sit down and shut up and don't move, and then the things in your mind begin to come out of their holes and start doing their running around and singing and so forth, and if you just let that happen, you make contact with it.

NYQ: Is that something like what Buddhism calls the *erasure of the self?*

SNYDER: That's one kind of erasure of the self. That's the simplest kind, where the conscious mind temporarily relinquishes its self-importance, its sense of self-importance, of direct focus and decision making and lets peripheral and lower and in some sense deeper aspects of the mind begin to manifest themselves.

What I'm describing I think is common to the creative process for all kinds of people, and all kinds of arts, and they arrive at it not necessarily by formal practice of meditation, but by practice of an intuitive capacity to open the mind and to not cling to too rigid a sense of the conscious self.

NYQ: You have any number of poems—specifically, say, "Shark Meat"—which seem to pull everything together; in fact the very ending of "Shark Meat" speculates that this shark has crisscrossed and has been here before and has now come back to be with us. Is that something like a healing process? Is that what you had in mind in that poem?

SNYDER: In that poem, yes, on not so intense a level. I find it always exciting to me, beautiful, to experience the interdependencies of things, the complex webs and networks by which everything moves, which I think are the most beautiful awarenesses that we can have of ourselves and of our planet. Let me quote something:

> The Buddha once said, bhikshus, if you can understand this blade of rice, you can understand the laws of interdependence and origination. If you can understand the laws of interdependence and origination, you can understand the Dharma. If you understand the Dharma, you know the Buddha.

And again, that's one of the worlds that poetry has taken, is these networks, these laws of interdependence—which are not exactly the laws that science points out. They are—although they are related—but imagination, intuition, vision clarify them, manifest them in certain ways—and to be able to transmit that to others is to transmit a certain quality of truth about the world.

NYQ: There are times when what you've been writing has been what would obviously be called *poetry,* and other times you convey that in what would ordinarily be called *prose*—would you try to explore the border between poetry and prose in your expression, or would you regard those as two separate things?

SNYDER: You are thinking of the essays in *Earth House Hold?*

NYQ: *Earth House Hold* and *The Back Country.* "Why Tribe," for example, is something like that.

SNYDER: Well, *Back Country,* I guess, is really all poetry, to my notion, and *Earth House Hold* is all prose, to my notion. But it's a thin line sometimes. The first difference is that (this is me speaking of my own sense of my own prose) that what I call prose does not have the musical phrase or the rhythm behind it. Nor does it have the content density or the complexity,

35

although the complexity of some of the writing in *Earth House Hold* is fairly—it is fairly complex sometimes. I don't really think of them as different so much as—I adopt whatever structure seems to be necessary to the communication in mind. And I try to keep a clear line between, say, notebook journals, journal jottings and poems—and again, the real line is in the music and the density—although again, to be fair, not all my poems are necessarily that dense in terms of content analysis, but have maybe a musical density sometimes.

What I might add to that is this: I seem to write very different poems. All of the poems that are most interesting to me are different from each other, almost all of them. And I see them almost as different, each one different form and a different strategy for dealing with a different impulse, and different communication.

There's another level—in the longer loop—we've been talking about short loops now—but in the longer loop I have some concerns that I'm continually investigating that tie together biology, mysticism, prehistory, general systems theory, and my investigations in these things cause me to hit different new centers in interrelationships, different interstices in those networks of ideas and feelings, and when I hit those interstices, sometimes a poem comes out of there, and that's a different place. Each one of them is a different face, many-faceted, of whatever it is I'm trying to work around.

NYQ: The ones you've just described seem to be intellectual, as opposed to emotional concerns.

SNYDER: Yes. Those are emotional-intellectual concerns! Again, they shade off. Like, it's the sanctity or the sacredness of all sentient beings as an emotional concern. The richness and the diversity of all sentient beings and the necessity for the survival of the gene pool for this to continue to be interesting is a biological concern. They shade over into each other.

NYQ: You were talking a couple of minutes ago about activities like logging and pole-skinning—well, you have come to the *NYQ* office by subway. You're giving a poetry reading at the 92nd Street Y tonight. How can you reconcile—how do you manage to put this all together—staying close to what presumably are the sources of your inspiration, like the back country, like these activities, with what a poet has got to do, giving readings and bothering with publishers and being interviewed like this?

SNYDER: Well, I don't find it particularly contradictory, but then contradictions don't bother me. Giving poetry readings is part of my work, because the poem lives in the voice, and I do it not just for money, although that certainly is a consideration, but because I feel this is where I get to try my poems out and I get to share a little bit of what my sense of the music of them is with others. And I wouldn't feel right if I didn't do that. The poem has to be sung once in a while. To travel around the country is a pleasant luxury, which may not be possible much longer as the whole transportation system will get increasingly expensive and nervous, but as long as it's possible, I'll indulge myself in it and what I gain from that is keeping in touch with the whole amazing network of American intellectual life and seeing many levels of things happening all the time, which I have no objection to seeing, you know. That's part of one's education and keeping one's level of awareness up. Living in the country for me is not a retreat, it's simply placing myself at a different point in the net, a different place in the network, which does not mean that I'm any less interested in the totality of the network, it's simply that's where I center myself.

NYQ: If you lived in the city, do you think you would write very differently from the way you write?

SNYDER: Probably not too differently, especially as I'm learning to see cities as natural objects. I'm getting better able to see what is natural and what is musical.[4]

NYQ: You're stressing finding your own voice, your own identity. Does it help? Has it helped you? Would you recommend that others study with other poets?

SNYDER: Yes. I feel very strongly that poetry also exists as part of a tradition, and is not simply a matter of only private and personal vision, although sometimes something very remarkable comes out of that kind of spontaneous and sort of untutored singing. There are several things that are more universal that we must tap into before personal utterances can become truly poems. One level is the very level of the language and its tradition of songs. We are immediately tied into a tradition by the very fact that we are dealing with the language, and the language is something with an enormous amount of history embedded in it—cultural history.

I feel that one should learn everything about poetry, that he should read everything that he can get his hands on, first from his own tradition and then from every other tradition that he has access to, to know *what* has been done, and to see *how* it has been done. That in a sense is true craft: that one learns by seeing what the techniques of construction were from the past and saves himself the trouble of having to repeat things that others have done that need not be done again. And then also he knows when he writes a poem that has never been written before.

I like to extend it out into other traditions for the very reason that we now are becoming totally cosmopolitan—we might as well do it. For me it's the Chinese tradition and the tradition of Indian vernacular poetry, and also classical Sanskrit poetry of India that I learned most from.

What parallels that is the inner level of universality which is in a sense the collective unconscious that belongs to more than your private self. When you touch on those deeply archetypal things in yourself and at the same time are in touch with what the generations before you have done with the same kind of impulses and the same depths of the mind, then you're able to steer a course with your own voice that will be a new creation, it seems to me. Without that drawing the cross between the personal unconscious to the collective unconscious and one's personal use of language into the collective use of language, you remain simply private. And poetry to be poetry has to speak from a deeper place than the private individual.

NYQ: One thing you've done is translation. *Cold Moun-*

tain Poems. Would you suggest to poets that they get into a fair amount of translating that way?

SNYDER: I'm not sure I would. Translation is too tempting, and I think as an exercise it's good, but it takes you away from yourself finally, from your own work. I think that too many poets take up translating—well, I shouldn't say this. *Some* poets take up translating because they seem to have run out of water in their own well. And maybe they should just keep digging at their own well instead of going over and borrowing it from somebody else's, which is what it seems to be.

Now the way I did the Han-shan translations was very much like what I described earlier. I stumbled on it, you know, that you could read what the Chinese said and then visualize what the Chinese, what the poem was, what the, quote, *"poem"* was, as Robert Duncan would say, the poem that's back there, and see that clear enough to then write down the poem in English directly, then look at the English and check it again against the Chinese and—to make sure that they really weren't too out of line.[5]

NYQ: Do you make it a practice to meet with other poets, poets who have either an affinity for the kind of content, or the kind of resource—like Jerome Rothenberg, for example—do you make it a point to meet with a lot of people that way?

SNYDER: No, I don't make a point of it. One needs a lot of solitude, a lot of silence, to work. I met a lot of poets in the fifties, and we nourished each other in a grand way. We needed each other and we became a small, quote, "culture," warm and moist and nourishing—and we grew out of that, and I—

That was a particularly deep culture of San Francisco for me at that time, and my contact with, first of all, Kenneth Rexroth, my teacher of Chinese poetry Ch'en Shih-hsiang, Philip Whalen, Lew Welch, Michael McClure, Philip Lamantia, Robert Duncan, and other poets of that time—

NYQ: No women?

SNYDER: Not right then. There weren't any that were part of the, quote, "culture," that was nourishing itself—not as writers, not that I can recollect. Diane Wakoski a little later, a year or two later. Diane was a very young barefoot girl in San Francisco then, and she began writing, and a little bit later Joanne Kyger came into that, and she's still writing poetry. She and I were married for a while.

But I'm thinking of that initial period. There was indeed a great need for each other, and I have much gratitude for that. *Now,* to the contrary, I think that poets perhaps place too much importance—and writers in general—on seeing each other, meeting each other, talking with each other, going to one person's house, going back to the other's house, and then saying, "When shall I see you again," "Well, let's meet again Wednesday," and then doing it again on Wednesday and—

Poetry is not a social life. Nor is it a career. It's a vocation. To be a careerist and to make a social life out of poetry is to waste the best of your opportunities, probably, for doing your work.

NYQ: You don't teach?

SNYDER: No. I have taught. I taught a year once. And I like to teach.

NYQ: You did like it?

SNYDER: Oh yes, except you have to talk too much! It's such a verbal activity, teaching at universities; it depends so much on language, just speech. Although it's getting better now. People feel forward enough to have silence in class sometimes, and undertake nonverbal or only semiverbal ways of teaching sometimes—experiential ways of teaching. There's something very good that's happening.

NYQ: Do you ever use words purely for the sound, the music, independent of the meaning of the word?

SNYDER: No. I like to think there is a merger of the sound and the meaning in some of the poems I have written. I try to steer a middle path in that.

NYQ: How about rhyme?

SNYDER: I use internal rhyme fairly frequently.

NYQ: Would you say that it just happens?

SNYDER: It just happens, yes.

40

NYQ: We got a note a few months ago from Charles Bukowski, who said that craft interviews remind him of people polishing mahogany. Do you have some response to that?

SNYDER: I like to polish mahogany! I like to sharpen my chain saw. I like to keep all my knives sharp. I like to change oil in the truck.

Creativity and maintenance go hand in hand. And in a mature ecosystem as much energy goes to maintenance as goes to creativity. Maturity, sanity, and diversity go together, and with that goes stability. I would wish that we could in time emerge from traumatized social situations and have six or seven hundred years of relative stability and peace. Then look at the kind of poetry we could write! Creativity is not at its best when it's a by-product of turbulence.

The great Zen masters, the great Chinese poets, some of the great landscape painters, and some of the great Buddhist philosophers, were all contemporaries over just a few centuries in the T'ang Dynasty. The whole power that comes out of that is the power of men who have achieved sanity of a working sort in a society which has a working peace, and then have said, "Now where do we go from here?" When we get to the top of the hundred-foot pole, keep going!

There are some equivalent things you can see in India, although India has a more turbulent history than China, I think. And finally, I intuit it as being the case, dialectically the case, so to speak.

NYQ: Would you say that a religious outlook is indispensable for the poet, for poetic creativity?

SNYDER: Not as such. I would say more, but the religious outlook would take us into a lot of tedious definitions. Spiritual curiosity, yes. Spiritual and psychological and personal curiosity. Curiosity about the world—yes, of course. Curiosity about consciousness, primarily, which is what you begin to be able to do when you sing.

NYQ: Do you think of your audience when you write?

SNYDER: Sure, I think of it more as my friends, family, community, my face-to-face social network. I don't abstract my au-

41

dience outside of what I see face to face. Now that comes to include many people around America whom I've seen face to face. I have a sense of who they are and—yes, I write to them. Sometimes at them, sometimes slightly over, but at least with them in mind.

NYQ: You said at one point that you felt you needed a great deal of solitude to write—

SNYDER: Not just to write, to live.

NYQ: Are you a seasonal poet? Do you write more in the fall than in the spring?

SNYDER: Well, the way I live right now, I guess I probably write more in the winter. Because in the spring I go out in the desert for a while, and I give a few readings, and then when I get back it's time to turn the ground over and start spring planting, and then right after that's done it's time to do the building that has to be done, and then when that's done, it's time to start cutting firewood, and then when the firewood's done, it's just about time to start picking apples and drying them, and that takes a couple of weeks to get as many apples as possible and dry them, and then at the end of the apple season I begin to harvest the garden, and a lot of canning and drying is done maybe, and then when that season passes, to chestnuts and picking up the wild grapes, and then I've got to put the firewood in, and as soon as I get the firewood in, hunting season starts—and that winds up about the end of October with Halloween festivities, and then I go East for a month to read. So December, January and February is my time of total isolation, writing; and I don't see anybody in those months.

NYQ: When you say solitude, do you mean literally alone?

SNYDER: Well, no, my family is with me, and there are neighbors to walk to. It's also during those months that we're most cut off, no electricity anywhere, no phone; the roads get snowed in and you can't get to my place. So the actual reading and writing is part of a seasonal process for me now. Although, of course, if you can get a poem going any time of the year, you'll do it—but to concentrate on that deeply, to get a lot of reading done, is a winter three-month chance.

NYQ: At the time you lived in Japan, did you have a similar cycle?

SNYDER: It was geared entirely to the cycle of the nearby Zen monastery. They have an annual cycle; it's like a farmer's cycle, that's all.

There's something about craft that we haven't touched on—I can't throw any light on it, really; I'd just like to suggest it as something to keep in mind, and that is: How do you go about—what kind of criteria do you employ—in feeling that a poem is well crafted? How do I feel when I feel a poem is well crafted? It's an extremely subtle thing, but part of it can be described in no other way than *taste*. There is an intuitive aesthetic judgment that you can make that in part spots phoniness, spots excess, spots the overblown, or the undersaid, the unripe, or the overripe, and feels its way out to what seems just right, and that balance is what I work for, just the right tone, just the right balance, for the poem to do just what I wanted it to do. Or I shouldn't phrase it that way—for the poem to be just what *it* wanted to be. Then it takes on a life of its own, and it loses no energy in the process.

NYQ: How is your work evolving now? Where is it going?

SNYDER: I'm still working, as I have for the last fifteen years, on one central long interconnected work in progress, with small poems being written peripheral to that.

NYQ: *Mountains and Rivers Without End?*

SNYDER: Right. Which is not an endless poem, it has an intention of being ended. But there's a lot of still relatively intractable material that I'm wrestling with, trying to punch it all up and drive it into the corral, and it takes time, because they keep sneaking back and I miss one—

KNOTS IN THE GRAIN

The following interview was given immediately after the "Craft Interview" with the New York Quarterly. *The interviewer is John Jacoby, of the English department at Southern Methodist University.*

JACOBY: This morning you were talking about the Shinto shrines placed near natural objects that vibrated with dense energy or special strength. I wonder about your sense of what poetic structures invoke or contain that kind of energy?

SNYDER: That reminds me of the Japanese term for song, *bushi* or *fushi,* which means a whorl in the grain. It means in English what we call a knot, like a knot in a board. It's a very interesting sense of song—like the grain flows along and then there's a turbulence that whorls, and that's what they call a song. It's an intensification of the flow at a certain point that creates a turbulence of its own which then as now sends out an energy of its own, but then the flow continues again. That's parallel to what Black Elk says in *Black Elk Speaks* talking of the Plains Indian view of physical nature: that trees, animals, mountains are in some sense individualized turbulence patterns, specific turbulence patterns of the energy flow that manifest themselves temporarily as discrete items, playing specific roles and then flowing back in again. I like to think of poetry as that, and as that, let's see, as the knot of the turbulence, whorl or a term that Pound was fond of from his friend Wyndham Lewis, "vortex." Or Yeats's term "gyre" too. In the flow of general language, in the flow of linguistic utterance—we live in a continuous stream of speech, of utterance, which is pretty much on the same level—the poem or the song manifests itself as a special concentration of the capacities of the language and rises up into its own shape. Now the question that people ask inevitably is, does this shape then mean a formal form, is that the shape it takes? And the question of course about premodern traditional English poetic forms as against what has been taking place the last few decades of the so-called free verse or open poetry. And the question is, are these formless—to which the answer is of course they're not formless.

Nothing is formless (*laughter*). Everything takes strict pattern including the flowing water in the stream which follows the physical laws of wave movement, or the physical laws by which clouds move, or gases move, or liquids move amongst each other, or liquids of different temperatures interchange. All these things are form, but there is more or less fluidity in the form, and there is also the possibility that the formal patterning is to be found in a longer range measuring periodicity than is provided by our traditional ways of patterning. Metrics and stanzas are matters of periodicity, establishing recurrences, and those established recurrences take place in very short lengths, like one line at a time: iambic pentameter, whatever it is. You can get longer reaches of periodicity, but in English prosody they're fairly short range structurings. I wouldn't have thought of a language to talk about longer potential structurings if I hadn't come on to the music of India and in the music of India the structure of *raga,* melodic mode, and *tala,* rhythmic mode, by which very lengthy compositions are established, and then within that, within certain structural terms improvised. These give me a model that I understand in my own work to be parallel, analogous in some senses to my own work, of a longer range sense of structuring with improvisatory possibilities taking place on a foundation of a certain steadiness that runs through it. So one poem has of itself the whole periodicity of one line, one structuring, and a number of poems to get a scene together will form a construct which is like one whole melodic thing. The

45

model that underlies that also is the sense of the melodic phrase as dominating the poetic structure, a kind of sense of melodic phrase as forming the poem rather than some formal metric stanza pattern that belongs to the past.

JACOBY: I've encountered some new formal patterns in your poems recently like the mantra or the chant that are unfamiliar to me. Do you think of those as being different from the western forms?

SNYDER: Well, the use of mantra . . . I haven't done that in too many poems. Which ones are you thinking of?

JACOBY: "A Curse/On the men in Washington, Pentagon."

SNYDER: Yes, that's a little bit of an example of imprecatory magic. It isn't really much, I don't think, a part of my poetics. In "Smokey the Bear Sutra" there's a mantra and in "Spel Against Demons" there's again the same mantra. That's a very specific kind of use of it. I haven't taken it any farther than that—except in a long poem called "The Circumambulation of Mt. Tamalpais." Well then, that's a pure mantric poem. It's full of chanting, and on the occasions when I chant it why that does a very special thing with everybody. That's the one place where I took that whole mantric thing by the horns and used it, but what I'm more interested in now is formulating some mantric possibilities within the English language, within the English phrasings.

JACOBY: I hear that in "No Matter, Never Mind," "Without," "Charms." They remind me of Anglo-Saxon riddles, something that old.

SNYDER: (*Deep laugh.*) Yes, there's a little bit of that in that. There's also . . . in a few recent poems I've gotten directly into song or using fragments of song within the poem. One of the things I'll read tonight does that, has that power and that concentration, one called "Magpie's Song." The key line in it is (*sings*):

> *Here in the mind, brother,*
> *Turquoise blue.*
> *Here in the Mind, Brother,*
> *Turquoise Blue*

46

Like that. That's . . . it sets the tone for that. Or another one called "Tomorrow's Song," of which the end song is a little chorus that goes like this (*sings*):

> *in the service*
> *of the wilderness*
> *of life*
> *of death*
> *of the Mother's breasts!*
> *in the service*
> *of the wilderness*
> *of life*
> *of Death*
> *of the Mother's breasts!*

I'm playing with that.

JACOBY: Do you have a sense of where a new stylistic potential, like the use of song, comes from? Why is that here now and not . . .

SNYDER: Well, I've always sung songs. One of my earliest poetic educations was a deep and loving listening to American folksongs. Going way back . . . I got all the Library of Congress records when I was a youngster and I listened to all the early . . . before anybody had heard of Leadbelly, I was listening to him and learning songs, and playing the guitar, and singing folksongs. I can sing about two hundred folksongs by heart, and I used to do that at hootenannies. But it never surfaced in my poetry before. That was one of those foundations that you lay, that you don't use till later, till you're ready. But I don't think I quite saw or I didn't feel the way to use it until I got more into a feeling for the music of India, the poetry of India, and the use of song in Indian poetry, East Indian poetry. I have a good sense of the poetry and music of India, partly because my wife, Masa, is a dancer, and her dance is Bharat Natyam, the classical dance of South India. She has a lot of that music around the house and we listen to it all the time. It fills our lives.

JACOBY: That leads me to another question I wanted to ask about rhythm. I remember when *Riprap* came out I'd seen a prose statement that said that the rhythms of the poems came from the rhythms of the physical labor, or riprapping, and the other work described. Now that you're not doing physical labor, do you have similar places to catch rhythms from?

SNYDER: Well, it's a mistake to assume that I'm not doing physical labor.

JACOBY: If you built your own house, I guess it is . . .

SNYDER: I not only built my own house, I do everything else around it continually. I'm farming all the time: cutting six cords of firewood for the winter, planting fruit trees, putting in fencing, taking care of the chickens, maintenance on the car, and maintenance on the truck, doing maintenance on the road. There's an enormous amount of physical work to be done.

That's a kind of work rhythm to be sure . . . which is just good old rural life work rhythms. Though I think probably the rhythm I'm drawing on most now is the whole of the landscape of the Sierra Nevada, to feel it all moving underneath. There is the periodicity of ridge, gorge, ridge, gorge, ridge, gorge at the spur ridge and tributary gorges that makes an interlacing network of, oh, 115-million-year-old geological formation rhythms. I'm trying to feel through that more than anything else right now. All the way down to some Tertiary gravels which contain a lot of gold from the Pliocene. Geological rhythms. I don't know how well you can do that in poetry. Well, like this for example. Have you ever tried singing a range of mountains?

JACOBY: No.

SNYDER: Do you know how you do it?

JACOBY: No.

SNYDER: Well, you sit down somewhere where you're looking at a long mountain horizon. Then you sing it up and down all the way along like that.

I tried it on the mountains up above Death Valley, the Panamint range, one time. I tried it many times until I got it right. You know, until I got to know that skyline so well that I knew when I was following the melody that the mountains were making. At first it was hit or miss kind of. And then you get closer. Then you begin to feel it. Then you get so that it's a kind of a source of form, right?

JACOBY: Right. I want to ask a nonformal question. I noticed in some of the new poems that they get scarier, maybe more angry. I'm thinking of "White Devils."

SNYDER: Oh, there are a few like that.

JACOBY: You talk about a poet needing to know the beings that inhabit his unconscious—know how to meet them. I wonder if you'd say something about that.

SNYDER: Well, I don't want to say too much about it because that belongs to the oral transmission, mind to mind, poet to poet, transmission of how you deal with demons (*laughs*), but we have to learn to do that quite clearly. And for some reason having demons seems to be one of the occupational hazards of being creative—more for some people and less for others.

JACOBY: I'd like to talk about the anger that is more political, as in "A Curse/On the men in Washington, Pentagon" or "The Call of the Wild." Does that anger come out of a political position?

SNYDER: Yes it does. My political position is to be a spokesman for wild nature. I take that as a primary constituency. And for the people who live in dependence on that, the people for whom the loss of that would mean the loss of their livelihood, which is Paiute Indians, Maidu Indians, Eskimos, Bushmen, the aborigines of New Guinea, the tribesmen of Tibet, to some extent the Kurds, people all over the world for whom that's their livelihood. That's a kind of politics, right? In the service of the wilderness, in the service of the Great Goddess Artemis.

That comes to me naturally, that position. It's not an anti-human position. It's a position simply of advocacy, taking the role of being the advocate for a realm for which few men will stand up. Someone must be a spokesman for that, and I think that poets are better prepared to be the spokesmen for that than most people are, particularly someone with the background of myself.

JACOBY: That puts you in a position of being a spokesman in the land of the enemy.

SNYDER: Yes. Which is all right. A spokesman in the society of the enemy, but the land is my friend. I have supporters all around me, trees, and birds, and so forth, and also a lot of people. You know, it's also the land of the American Indian.

JACOBY: In about 1960 you said the structure of *Mountains and Rivers Without End* followed a certain type of Noh play. I wonder if you've held to that or if as new kinds of structuring have come to you, been used in your other poems, you've also changed your sense of structure of *Mountains and Rivers*.

SNYDER: Well, I haven't exactly changed it, but I've deepened my sense of the possible . . . the multiplicity of levels. The Noh play is certainly a key structural sense of it with the scroll itself an analogous structuring moving across the landscape, moving through different realms, moving through different seasons, but coming to a kind of ambiguous end sometimes. It's hard to speak about *Mountains and Rivers* because it's a rather complex project. I haven't entirely visualized it. I'm not trying to entirely visualize it. When I get into the last lap of the work it will finally come clear. Just as my *Myths and Texts* finally came clear in the last lap. So I'm working toward that still.

JACOBY: There's an amazing range of knowledge in it.

SNYDER: It's not that much knowledge. Hopefully, when the poem is completed it will be self-informing to a degree that the individual sections are not now . . . that they will reinforce each other, and reverberate, and echo in such a way that people will have a clearer sense of what's involved. Also I hope to . . . well, I'm considering writing a little poem for the appendix which will be a glossary and footnotes poem. A poem in footnotes. I'm toying with that possibility if it seems necessary.

JACOBY: We're just about at the end of the time you promised, and I wonder if as a kind of close you'd comment on the energy crisis and what that means to you as a poet.

SNYDER: It doesn't mean anything to me personally as a poet because it won't change my way of life.

JACOBY: Not even the pressure to be political?

SNYDER: Everything is going to be new politics now. It's all going to be energy politics. Everything is going to be redrawn. The realignments of the nations of the world according to their access to energy is now taking place. Everybody thought it was money that counted before. Now it turns out that the only real wealth is oil. That is real wealth. You can't burn money—I mean you can't get much heat out of it when you burn it. You can light a cigar with it, and that's about all. So oil is now the real wealth, fossil fuels. The actual "real wealth" is knowing how to get along "without." Now which of those is the real wealth? "Do more with less," as the slogan goes. In other words, human mind-energy capacities, human intelligence capacities as against mechanical and fossil-fuel-fired capacities. This is a marvelous time in which the nations of the world may get a new balance and a perspective on themselves—if it doesn't degenerate into hysteria and short range crisis thinking. If we rush into a crisis mentality—totalitarian and draconian measures to keep the cars running, and the houses heated to seventy-two degrees, and the GNP continually growing—then we will rip off nature. We should try to allay anxiety and spread confidence in the natural beauty of the human mind and the natural dignity of life at its normal, natural, ancient, slower pace. I think that creative people, poets, religious people, if they wish to speak, have a message which is of great value now . . . although whether or not anyone will heed it is another question.

JACOBY: Right. Reminds me of the last stanza of "The Call of the Wild":

> *I would like to say*
> *Coyote is forever*
> *Inside you.*
>
> *But it's not true.*

SOUTH INDIAN POETRY AND DANCE

Gary Snyder gave the following talk in February, 1976, at a benefit poetry reading for the Balasaraswati Dance Company. The reading was opened with a brief dance by his wife. Masa Snyder began dancing Bharat Natyam in 1968 and has studied intensively at various times since 1972 with Balasaraswati.

I want to talk about South India and the poetic tradition, the dance. I'm not an expert on this and I might get some of it wrong but I sense South India to have been, for a period, one of those few totally solid, integrated civilizations in which for a time everything was moving together with great beauty and force, when minds were really dancing together. T'ang China was a place like that, Damascus in the twelfth century was another.

The people of South India are Dravidian-speaking, not Indo-Aryan; indigenous perhaps, certainly much earlier in India than the Indo-Aryan invaders who came down around 1500 B.C. (cowboys with wagons and domesticated cows and horses; speaking their own languages and ours too, lighter skinned). The Dravidian people have very dark skin—sometimes a blue-black sheen to it, with narrow, delicate Caucasoid-like bone structure. Their early traditions refer to a preliterate period of poet-singers called *Pānar*—the word *pān* meaning music, actually same meaning as North Indian raga.

These men and women, as specialists, inherited the most archaic magical and mythical traditions, and were employed as singers and dancers for festivals and all sorts of magical occasions, such as battles! In South India they had musicians and drummers play music when there was a battle going on, and pitch in flowers from time to time—for magical reasons, to help contain the chaos of warfare and death. So, early, dance was thought of as a mode of contacting the Sacred without it getting too chaotic and spilling over. The sense of the Sacred in ancient South India was that it is very scary, that it can sweep things away. You need to make contact with it, but you need an assured, disciplined, beautiful way to step toward it.

The *Pānar* poets and dancers are also the forerunners of the great Tamil classical Dravidian poetic tradition—the *Eight Anthologies, Kuruntokai,* which in writing survive to this time. There are a total of 2,400 poems in the *Eight Anthologies,* with 473 poets-with-names, and 102 anonymous poets—a major poetic tradition.

In Japan, as you know, haiku are always classified as belonging to one of the four seasons. Well, in the South Indian tradition it is more complex: they perceive their country to have five distinctive landscapes or habitats: mountain, forest, farmland, seacoast, and arid wasteland. Every poem belongs to one of these five landscapes, with a corresponding flower, tree, animal, type of love affair, and type of warfare. This whole body of images again splits down the middle into two categories called *akam* and *puram*—inner and outer. *Akam* poems deal with love, *puram* poems with warfare and the praise of kings.

The poems of the *Eight Anthologies* were created largely by a literate, court-connected group of men and women, specialists called *Puruvat* who had inherited, and socially upgraded, the traditions of the low-caste, wandering, nonliterate *Pānar*. The *Pānar* were the originators of the music of India, both north and south.

In medieval South India the Shaivite (Shiva-worshipping) and Vaishnava (Vishnu-worshipping) traditions came down from the north. A body of vernacular songs of praise to Shiva or Vishnu in his form of Krishna arose, which became assimilated to the older line of music and song. Bharat Natyam,

"Dance of Bharat," is the name given the final, polished synthesis of ancient, medieval, and diverse folk traditions of South India. It has been transmitted in its present form for centuries; you just saw a little introductory bud of it tonight.

Dance, music, poetry, architecture, temple design as mandala, religion, all coevolved. The people of Tamil Nadu used the language of music to talk about poetry or buildings, or the language of religion to talk about dance and song, or the aesthetic vocabulary of architecture to talk about religion. It became one solid fabric of very deep spiritual and meditative practice of daily life.

One flower of that is still alive, Bharat Natyam. The classical and vernacular South Indian poetic traditions are gone, and nobody's doing the architecture right now. The music and dance survive.

THE REAL WORK

Paul Geneson drove from his home in Boulder, Colorado, to California in the summer of 1976 to interview Snyder. The interview first appeared in the Ohio Review (*Fall 1977*).

GENESON: For you personally, what is the attraction of the rural life?

SNYDER: Well, apart from arguments about poetry, and *city* or *country,* it's obvious that city life has become difficult. It's *quite* obvious. And it's only natural that people should look for other ways to live. There is an implicit satisfaction in rural life, and in backcountry life—at least for some people. The pleasures are numerous and the work is hard, and one is literally less alienated from one's water, one's fuel, one's vegetables, and so forth. Those are fundamentals, those are ancient human fundamentals.

And it wouldn't be going too far to say that human creativity and all of the arts will begin to wither if they are pulled too far away from fundamentals of how people really should and have had to live, over millennia. We are, after all, an animal that was brought into being on this biosphere by these processes of sun and water and leaf. And if we depart too far from them, we're departing too far from the mother, from our own heritage.

The problem is, where do you put your feet down, where do you raise your children, what do you do with your hands. Now, working in a tanker with my body and with my hands in the engine room of a ship is in some ways less alienated than it would be to sit and look at this beautiful view, talking constantly on a telephone and typing on a typewriter and never *touching* it. It's the use of the *body* and the involvement of all the senses that is important at that point.

GENESON: What poets did you read when you were young that have influenced you?

SNYDER: A main progression of interests and influences would be: Carl Sandburg in early teens, and Edgar Lee Masters and some of the other Middle American poets, especially Sandburg, who's very beautiful for a kid, going directly into the poetry of D. H. Lawrence, which was a very powerful discovery for me when I was about seventeen.

[Sandburg's poems] are in a populist style, they're in a big spirit. They're in the sense of the city as the marketplace for the agriculture of the Plains. That's something real.

And Whitman, at the age, too. Then D. H. Lawrence. And from Lawrence into, on the one hand, Robinson Jeffers, whom I saw as a twentieth-century reverse image of Walt Whitman. And on the other hand into Eliot, Wallace Stevens, and Williams.

GENESON: How is Jeffers a "reverse image" of Whitman?

SNYDER: Well, Whitman was optimistic and Jeffers is pessimistic and they're talking about the same thing.

GENESON: About the land?

SNYDER: About the prophecy of America. They are the prophets of America, each in their own century.

GENESON: You mentioned Eliot—don't you find Eliot more of a *heady* poet?

SNYDER: What's really fun about Eliot is his intelligence and his highly selective and charming use of Occidental symbols which point you in a certain direction. I read *From Ritual to Romance,* and went on to read *Prolegomena to the Study of Greek Religion,* Jane Ellen Harrison, and it just kept pushing me back. It takes you all the way back to the cave at Trois Frères in France, ultimately. If you follow anything that has any meat to it it'll take you back there. And so Eliot, without maybe even consciously being aware of it, points us some profound directions. *Four Quartets* is my favorite Eliot work, and I think that it is a major work.

GENESON: Do you think that maybe Eliot, unknowingly, was Whitmanesque even as he was denying Whitman? I'm thinking of the sense of place in the *Quartets*—East Coker, the river?

SNYDER: But the way he uses that, it seems to me, is as symbol rather than for the *Ding an sich*. He uses it with irony and almost with contempt—not for itself but for what it means in his system of things. Which is all right. But it's a different use.

Now, Eliot is a ritualist, a very elegant ritualist of key Occidental myth-symbols with *considerable* grasp of what they were about: like Joyce was, in another way—they're working from slightly different positions. And I think that's what he was. With "The Dry Salvages" there's an almost pedantic voice of the ritualist coming through.

GENESON: How did Eliot influence your poetry?

SNYDER: Precision. I went from *From Ritual to Romance* to *The Mabinogion*—the ways that take you back to the archaic roots. He had the sense of the roots. He had the sense of the roots more deeply than Pound did, actually. Pound was never able to get back earlier than the Early Bronze Age. Olson at least gets to the Pleistocene.

GENESON: What do you mean when you say a modern poet can get back to the Pleistocene?

SNYDER: I mean their imagination is able to encompass it, that they feel that it's part of their lives, that they feel comradeship in connection with it, that they feel that there is humanity in that that speaks to them. This is part of our history.

GENESON: T. S. Eliot, the Anglo-Catholic?

SNYDER: Yes. As Anglo-Catholic, it's all right. The Catholic Church is full of people who did that—not *full,* but there were a number of them. The latest being Teilhard de Chardin, the best example, actually. I mean Catholic does mean catholic in the best sense, if they do it right.

GENESON: Some of the other poets who influenced you?

SNYDER: Okay, I was continuing my beginnings: Stevens, Eliot, Pound, Williams, and Yeats.

GENESON: Stevens's abstraction?

SNYDER: I just looked at it, that's all. I looked at it and I proceeded to toy with it. I'm not describing that as an influence, actually.

GENESON: Just people that you read?

SNYDER: People that I read and listened to closely. I listened to Gerard Manley Hopkins very closely.

GENESON: Because of his ear?

SNYDER: Because of the good sense he had of English and of the accentual line. And Yeats for his sense of symbol and imagery. And Pound for his peculiar ear. And after that I'm just out reading everything. But those are the ones I see as critical in my reading.

And then Chinese poetry—in translation, to begin with. And later Chinese poetry in Chinese.

Another body of material I ran onto that was extremely important to me was translations of American Indian song and myth in the Bureau of American Ethnology, Memoirs and Reports Series, which I started reading when I was around nineteen. Haida songs, Kwakiutl mythology—all of those things.

GENESON: Would you say that the study of anthropology per se is a little too dry?

SNYDER: If I were recommending anybody to study anything in the university over anything else, I would either recommend biology or anthropology. Anthropology is probably the most intellectually exciting field in the universities. The most *intellectually* exciting, the one where something's happening in *humanistic terms*. If you want to get exciting science, you go into biochemistry or something like that. But if you want to get interesting ideas you go into anthropology.

GENESON: In the genesis of the poem as you write it: do you take notes, or do these things just come to you? How does it arrive and what do you do first?

SNYDER: I listen to my own interior mind-music closely, and most of the time there's nothing particularly interesting happening. But once in a while I hear something which I recognize as belonging to the sphere of poetry. I listen very closely to that.

GENESON: Inside?

SNYDER: Inside. But it's coming from outside if you like.

GENESON: Are you talking about voices or ideas that are being directed at you? For example, your son might mention something about the creek that might trigger something—

SNYDER: I might hear that too, that's true. Prior to the writing of the poems I tend to have a sense of key areas that I'm watching that are beginning to evolve as points I must know about, that are beginning to evolve in my life. And poems will flow out of those in time. Now here's the list of things I want to watch right now. (*He opens a file drawer and takes out several cards.*) These three cards. That's how I identify things, by those little phrases. Part of my psychological and spiritual evolution is tied up with that. Out of that more precise language and symbol ultimately will come—more precise *music* will come.

*　　*　　*

GENESON: Do you have a special attachment to California?

SNYDER: My sense of place is the whole West Coast. No, not the whole West Coast, Northern California, Oregon and Washington are where I feel most at home. On the west slope. Plus the mountains. So this is a good place to live for me.

GENESON: And your advice to someone who grew up, say, in Cincinnati would be?

SNYDER: Learn about Cincinnati. It could be beautiful, Cincinnati could. This is what I tried to teach for two months: how to get to know Cincinnati. Which means, first of all, you have to get rid of the name *Cincinnati*.

GENESON: You suggested that?

SNYDER: Oh yes, of course, because after all it's the Ohio River Valley, really, that you're looking at. And *Ohio* means *beautiful* in Shawnee. And there you go, you start going back and connecting with all those loops.

GENESON: Did you feel people found that rather surprising? Or did they little by little come to accept that idea?

SNYDER: I think that they began to get a handle on why I was doing it after a while. It didn't seem quite right to them at first, though.

GENESON: Can you conceive of a person being a good teacher of poetry?

SNYDER: I like the apprentice relation as a way to go for that. I think that young people who want to have a teacher should not look at a university as a university, but look for the teacher. If the teacher happens to be a professor in the university, that's all right. But if not, not. In either case you go to that person directly, not to the administration building, and you say, "I want to be your student. What do I have to do?" And in doing that you expand the relationship into something more *personal,* more *menial,* more *direct.*

The model for that, for me, is the Japanese potters who take apprentices. And the thing that the apprentice first learns how to do is mix clay. Or Japanese carpentry apprentices who will spend months learning how to sharpen chisels and planes before they ever touch the tools to do work. You could learn as much from a good mechanic and how parts go together, and how you move and what goes in what order—

GENESON: Are you talking about poetry?

SNYDER: I'm talking about poetry. You learn how to use your mind in the act of handling parts and working. You learn how to work. You learn how things go together.

GENESON: You're making an analogy here.

SNYDER: But it's a *true* analogy. A master is a master. If you saw a man who was a master mechanic you'd do better—say you wanted to be a poet, and you saw a man that you recognized as a master mechanic or a great cook. You would do better, for yourself as a poet, to study under that man than to study under another poet who was not a master, that you didn't recognize as a master.

GENESON: Who was not a true poet?

SNYDER: Not only a true poet but a master—a *real* craftsman.

60

There are true poets who can't teach because they're hooked onto inspiration, spontaneity, voice, language—they do it but they're not grounded in details. They don't *really* know the materials. A carpenter, a builder knows what Ponderosa pine can do, what Douglas fir can do, what incense cedar can do and builds accordingly. You can build some very elegant houses without knowing that, but some of them aren't going to work, ultimately.

And so, I'm saying that behind the scenes there is the structural and the fundamental knowledge of materials in poetry, and learning from a master mechanic would give you some of those fundamentals as well as studying from an academician, say.

GENESON: It sounds as if you're talking more about an Oriental or an Eastern kind of mechanic, someone who is more sensitive, or *sensitized*.

SNYDER: No. I use the term master mechanic because I know a master mechanic, Rod Coburn. Whenever I spend any time with him, I learn something from him.

GENESON: About?

SNYDER: About *everything*. But I see it in terms of my craft as a poet. I learn about my craft as a poet. I learn about what it really takes to be a craftsman, what it really means to be committed, what it really means to work. What it means to be *serious* about your craft and no bullshit. Not backing off any of the challenges that are offered to you. You know, like not being willing to read books, for Christ's sake. You run into people who want to write poetry who don't want to read anything in the tradition. That's like wanting to be a builder but not finding out what different kinds of wood you use.

GENESON: When a person teaches poetry, ought he to talk about inspiration?

SNYDER: Inspiration is something that can be talked about, but can't be taught in the university context. What you *can* point out is that inspire has the word *spirit* in it, and is related to *ex*spire, *re*spire, and *con*spire. And point out a few other connections like that. I would say, offhand, if you want inspiration the two simplest and best ways to get it are to go on a long walking trip by yourself, or take a sweatbath. This will inspire you for poetry. Sweatbaths, especially.

GENESON: And did you tell your students this? Did you do any of this together?

SNYDER: Well, you see, the facilities aren't there. Now if I were teaching a poetry course at the university and I had everything I needed, there would have to be a sauna right there, and a quarter of an acre of garden plot, and a good kitchen, and some musical instruments and God knows what-all. That was what Philip Whalen said years ago when they asked him to teach a poetry workshop at Berkeley. Philip stated his demands: it would have to have a pump-organ and a kitchen—in the classroom. Because how can you teach poetry without at least those things? (*Spontaneous laughter.*) So, we're in harmony, Phil and I are, on that one.

GENESON: Kerouac talks a lot about the idea of spontaneity: the "spontaneous get with it," the "spontaneous recall of the unconscious." Do you also feel that way about composing poetry?

SNYDER: It's only part of it. The spontaneity is beautiful, and Jack's haiku, in *Mexico City Blues,* are some of the prettiest poems in the English language. But to complete the work of poetry as I see it in our time, here, I'd like to see some instantly-apprehended because so-well-digested larger loopings of lore. Now, if you haven't digested it and it hasn't become part of you, then you are looking things up in your library books. Or, as Philip Whalen says, in your Handbook of Comparative Mythology to look for the symbols to put in. That, of course, is wrong. But if you've absorbed and apprehended and digested it, why your apprehensive, pre-hensive mass that you can draw on is very large and very beautiful. This is part of the training you come in there with. Your spontaneity, in other words, can be very rich.

GENESON: But it's a prior experience that makes it rich?

SNYDER: That's right. That's really what we mean by learning and by being cultured—that the time process really does enrich and deepen what you have at hand at any time. And there's a point where you have enough at hand at any time and you're so comfortable with it that you can really turn some very rich thing out. That's what a great potter is.

GENESON: Do you feel the university has a function beyond what Allen Ginsberg feels is its importance—cataloguing?

SNYDER: Well, that's a great value of it. But in fact the university also has the function of reassessing our tradition, our body of lore, every generation. And in the process sometimes discovering things that were missed before and bringing them back to our attention—like Blake was brought to us, or like Melville's poetry was brought to us—that might have been lost otherwise. So the English department is a cardboard box that everybody throws every poetry magazine that comes in the mail into and says, "Well, we'll look at that later. I haven't got time to read it now." It's a backward function in time. Like some kinds of academic and intellectual pursuits are forward-looking —most of the sciences are looking for new breakthroughs, new discoveries. An English department is looking backward in time, trying to understand what happened as they go—you know, looping backward as they go, and trying to connect.

So they're establishing the tradition and that is their value. And I respect that. I have great respect for that. I don't think that they *understand* their function enough to have enough pride or enough pleasure in their work, though. And that's what makes me sad. They don't have a *tribal* sense of their own work, and it is a truly tribal work.

GENESON: What would you suggest to them?

SNYDER: I suggest that they get an anthropological and a prehistoric perspective on these things and then they'll see where what they're doing fits into the picture. And how the professors in the English department are like kiva priests, priests of the kiva that we have to go to from time to time to say, "Now why was it that there are three lines painted at the top of this eagle feather, with a little bit of red fluff on it. Now what was the reason for doing that?" Somebody who keeps that in mind for us.

It doesn't mean that they have to care a lot about it. But they do have to care about their role, about their function. And their function is maybe to tell some young guy who's going to be a beautiful poet or a beautiful dancer, to give him that one little extra bit of information to deepen what he's doing.

Because, you know, they carry the lore, they bear it. And they bear it for the benefit of the dancers who get inspired out there in the plaza.

In earlier times the English professor would have also been the raconteur, the storyteller who would, to a small select audience of students after the storytelling was over and the audience had gone home, tell them some of the *inner* meanings, some of the *background,* some of the *professional secrets* of what he had just recited. He doesn't have to be the poet who made it up necessarily, see?

GENESON: What has been your own relationship with the academy?

SNYDER: I went to Reed College in Oregon, I had some marvelous teachers, I learned how to use a library, I was in an atmosphere that challenged me and pushed me to the utmost, which was just what I needed. They wouldn't tolerate bullshit, made me clean up my prose style, exposed me to all varieties of intellectual positions and gave me a territory in which I could speak out my radical politics and get arguments and augmentations on it. It was an intensive, useful experience.

And also it was an intense enough education that I perceived that I would have to de-educate myself later. An education is only valuable if you're willing to give as much time to de-educating yourself as you gave to educating yourself. So, you go to college for four years, you have to figure you're going to do four years of coming off of it, too.

GENESON: When you say "de-educate yourself," you mean what?

SNYDER: I mean get back in touch with people, with ordinary things: with your body, with the dirt, with the dust, with anything you like, you know—the streets. The streets or the farm, whatever it is. Get away from books and from the elite sense of being bearers of Western culture, and all that crap. But also, ultimately, into your mind, into *original mind* before any books were put into it, or before any language was invented.

GENESON: You just mentioned that the professors were the bearers of the lore—

SNYDER: And the *best* professors, the best priests of the kiva are the ones who are able to show you the path out the door where there isn't any lore.

GENESON: And this is what you call the postuniversity experience?

SNYDER: It's what you call higher education. (*He laughs.*)

GENESON: Some people would say to a young poet, "Poetry is self-expression. Sit down and write what you can whenever you can." Would you say that?

SNYDER: No, I wouldn't say that. I don't think that's true. I think that poetry is a social and traditional art that is linked to its past and particularly its language, that *loops* and draws on its past and that serves as a vehicle for contact with the depths of our own unconscious—and that it gets better by practicing. And that the expression of self, although it's a nice kind of energy to start with, would not make any expression of poetry per se.

We all know that the power of a great poem is not that we felt that person expressed himself well. We don't think that. What we think is, "How deeply *I* am touched." That's our level of response. And so a great poet does not express his or her self, he expresses *all* of our selves. And to express *all* of ourselves you have to go beyond your own self. Like Dōgen, the Zen master, said, "We study the self to forget the self. And when you forget the self, you become *one* with all things." And that's why poetry's not self-expression in those small self terms.

GENESON: Japan plays a considerable role in your poetry. Would you say to a young poet, "Go to Japan"?

SNYDER: Good heavens no. What Japan as advice implies is: if there's a spiritual path that you feel is important to you, go out and study it, no matter where it leads. And the other thing that implies is: if you have the will and the energy and the opportunity, go live in an alien culture for awhile. It really does, as they say, "broaden" you. (*He laughs.*)

I like the way Jack Spicer saw it where all pure and true poetry is ultimately inspired in origin. It comes to us as a voice from outside. To even say that it comes from within is to mislead yourself. So we are the vehicle of that voice. However, if we are people who can hear that voice, then we should strive to be the best possible vehicle of that voice we can. Which means to learn other languages, to become as broadly human and as well-informed and aware as we can because that will give strength to our handling and expressing the power of the voice.

GENESON: Including translations?

SNYDER: Including translations. Reading. Learning how to *do* translations.

GENESON: Wallace Stevens said that the translator is a parasite. Do you agree with that?

SNYDER: We need everyone who can do it. Any good translator is a great help to all of us. A translator's no more a parasite than an interpreter standing at the edge of the creek helping a group of Crow and a group of Hunkpapa Sioux do some trading is a parasite—it's a valuable function. A translator is a valuable switch in an energy exchange flow.

GENESON: Apart from Oriental poets, what other poets have you read? Have you read many Spanish poets?

SNYDER: In translation.

GENESON: Neruda?

SNYDER: Vallejo.

GENESON: Which of these non-English poets that you've read in translation are especially interesting to you?

SNYDER: I'm not overwhelmingly moved by any one given poet in Spanish. I look at them. But I don't make fine distinctions. The only poets outside the English tradition that I make fine distinctions in my choices about are in Chinese, Japanese, and to some extent in the East Indian languages. The rest I just read.

GENESON: Do you think more people ought to study Chinese and Japanese? Do we need more translations of these poets?

SNYDER: I don't know if we *need* them. Yes, they'd be nice. There's a tremendous amount of poetry in Chinese that hasn't even been translated—I'm not sure it's all that good. Good translations of Tu Fu, whom the Chinese themselves consider their greatest poet and who undoubtedly must be one of the greatest poets of the world, are yet to come. Understanding the aesthetics of Japanese poetry is a marvelous exercise, also.

I quote to you one of Bashō's disciples who took down something Bashō once said to a group of students. He said, "To learn about the pine, go to the pine. To learn about bamboo, go to the bamboo. But this *learn* is not just what you think learn is. You only learn by becoming totally absorbed in that which you wish to learn. There are many people who think that they have learned something and willfully construct a poem which is artifice and does not flow from their delicate entrance into the life of another object."

GENESON: So when Sartre, the Western philosopher, goes to the tree, touches the tree trunk and says, "I feel in an absurd position—I cannot break through my skin to get in touch with this bark, which is outside me," the Japanese poet would say what?

SNYDER: Sartre is confessing the sickness of the West. At least he's honest.

The Oriental will say, "But there are ways to do it, my friend. It's no big deal." It's no big deal, especially if you get attuned to that possibility from early in life. There's something where, say, the American Indians and the Japanese are right on the same spot. They both know that that's possible, and that it is a major mode of knowledge—to learn about the pine from the pine rather than from a botany textbook. They know that that's right. They also know that you can look at the botany textbook and learn a few things, too.

GENESON: You mention in *Turtle Island* the idea of being in touch with the land, and the Indian myths of the land. In other places you use the Oriental teachings that you've personally experienced. How do you link these two?

SNYDER: Oh, it's all one teaching. There is an ancient teach-

67

ing, which we have American Indian expressions of, and Chinese, Tibetan, Japanese, Indian, Buddhist expressions of. And other expressions in the world. Each of us, according to our own needs and nature, can draw up the criteria for what expression suits us best, and what *practice* suits us best out of that. We will prefer some to others. There may be some lines of teaching which are really a little wrongheaded. So I would not argue that all paths necessarily lead to the same goal—I think some paths go to other places. But there is a body of paths which do come to the same goal—some with a more earthly stress, some with a more spiritual stress. But what they share in common is the exploration of consciousness itself: self-understanding, transcendence of self.

Native American people have many paths, many varieties in their paths, so you can't even speak of all of that as one. But they have, throughout Turtle Island, an ancient and clarified sense of what a right path is. And some of those societies, not all of them maybe, were actually living like a Zen monastery—a whole society *on the way*. Which is preferable to a fragmented, monastic transmission. A whole social transmission is more to be desired than a monastic and esoteric transmission.

GENESON: Do you still feel that a certain tribalism is implicit, or latent, in the culture?

SNYDER: Whatever we mean by that. Tribalism is I guess what we mean in suggesting that there's an alternative to the fragmented and alienated kind of social fabric we have now which lacks community and lacks communication. So yes, that's one of the things we hope for—still.

GENESON: So the subculture which had its roots in the sixties is not something you're pessimistic about even today?

SNYDER: No, because the subculture had its roots 40,000 years ago.

GENESON: We're not talking about fads then?

SNYDER: We're *not* talking about fads. To the contrary—the subculture is the main line and what we see around us is the anomaly.

GENESON: In *Turtle Island:* when you talk about the subculture, are you talking about myths of the land? A rediscovery of Indian lore? Or just a rediscovery of one's own humanity and a new set of myths?

SNYDER: Well, what's implied in the title is, first of all, not even a *re*discovery but a *dis*covery of North America—we haven't discovered North America yet. People live on it without knowing what it is or where they are. They live on it literally like invaders. You know whether or not a person knows where he is by whether or not he knows the plants. By whether or not he knows what the soils and waters do. Now that is so fundamental and basic, and so true that it's easy to overlook. There it is, it's not even arguable.

But we live in a nation of fossil fuel junkies, very sweet people and the best hearts in the world. But nonetheless fossil fuel junkies of tremendous mobility zapping back and forth, who are still caught on the myth of the frontier, the myth of boundless resources and a vision of perpetual materialistic growth. Now that is all very bad metaphysics, a metaphysics that is leading us to ruin. Turtle Island is *good* metaphysics because it points in the direction of real seeing. And the first step in real seeing is to throw out a European name and take a creative native name. And the second step is to erase arbitrary and nonexistent political boundaries from your mind and look at what the land really is, with mountain ridges, and rivers and tree zones and rain zones, and just keep going from there, you know, following those implications.

GENESON: And the cities?

SNYDER: And the cities are periodic tribal marketplaces.

GENESON: That people will be leaving or—

SNYDER: Well, they do all the time—they're coming and going all the time. Coming and going, coming and going. You know what cities really are? They're at the mouths of rivers, or at fords on rivers—hence *Ox*ford University. They're at access to trails which are passes over mountain ranges, they are transportation and exchange nodes, essentially, that have become stable and permanent. Or, the only other variety of city that counts, really, is a religious pilgrimage center, a city that evolves out of access to a sacred spot. Like Benares in India. Or like Jerusalem.

* * *

GENESON: As you see it, what is the function of poetry?

SNYDER: You ask me what is the function of poetry so I think, "What is the function of poetry since 40,000 years ago?" In all cultures of the world—total planetary overview. And in that sense the function of poetry is not only the intensification and clarification of the implicit potentials of the language, which means a sharpening, a bringing of more delight to the normal functions of language and making maybe language even work better since communication is what it's about. But on another level poetry is intimately linked to any culture's fundamental worldview, body of lore, which is its myth base, its symbol base, and the source of much of its values—that myth-lore foundation that underlies any society. That foundation is most commonly expressed and transmitted in the culture by poems, which is to say *by songs*. By songs that are linked to a dramatic or ritual performance much of the time. The oral tradition almost always puts its transmission into a form of measured language, which is easier to remember and can be chanted. Much of the world's lore has been transmitted, in one form or another, via poetic forms, measured language or sung language.

GENESON: One might argue that the world is just too large, that in order to have a campfire you'd have to have a *media* campfire. Would that be feasible?

SNYDER: Well, Marshall McLuhan tried to make the media into a tribal campfire. Since I'm not a person who has watched media much in my lifetime, I can't really speak with accuracy on that. I do think, though, that as we move, *of necessity,* toward some more decentralized and labor-intensive ways of working and living with each other, there will be a reemergence of community and neighborhood. And out of that, either in the city or in the country, a campfire circle, so to speak, reevolves. Any time any group of people in New York get together in somebody's apartment and read poems to each other, it's happening. Or get together to put on a play together, or make up a skit together, it's happening. It's the face-to-face working-it-out of the forms of the art with human beings that is real.

GENESON: W. H. Auden said about poetry that it won't change anything. Is that how you see poetry?

SNYDER: Ezra Pound said, to quote an oft-quoted line, that artists are the antennae of the race. How that probably functions in practice is that some people's sensibilities, as well as maybe their lifestyles, are out at the very edge of the unraveling cause-and-effect network of a society in time. And also are, by virtue of the nature of their sensibilities, tuned into other voices than simply the social or human voice. So they are like an early warning system that hears the trees and the air and the clouds and the watersheds beginning to groan and complain a little bit. And so they try to send a little bit of a warning back, although they themselves may not know what it is they're hearing. They also can hear the stresses and the fault block slippage creaking in the social batholith and also begin to give out warnings.

What proceeds on that is, for the poet in particular, a sense of the need to look at the key archetype image and symbol blocks and see if the blocks are working. Poetry effects change by fiddling with the archetypes and getting at people's dreams about a century before it actually effects historical change. A poet would be, in terms of the ecology of symbols, noting the main structural connections and seeing which parts of the symbol system are no longer useful or applicable, though everyone is giving them credence. And out of his own vision and hearing of voices he seeks for new paths for the mind-energy to flow, which would be literally more creative directions, but directions which change politics. Poets are more like mushrooms, or fungus—they can digest the symbol-detritus.

Thus, you proceed from an animistic idea that you can hear voices from trees. And a few decades later a lawyer, like Christopher Stone, writes a *legalistic* argument—"Should Trees Have Standing?"—arguing that trees should be involved in the democratic process. Now, where does it go from there? That is a myth-block idea in which a kind of language which is known to our whole culture—the rights of things, the potentiality of salvation of things—the idea is being turned around just a trifle. And it *catches* it a little. And you push it toward a generation or two in the future that can actually feel on a gut level that nonhuman nature has rights. And that will be the work of the poet, to set that direction.

GENESON: Some of the things you were writing in the fifties and sixties are just beginning to be talked about today: the preservation of the forests, and the whole general ecology, which seems to have reached near crisis—

SNYDER: Yes. But that's only one side of it. The work of poetry is really not the work of prophecy. Nor is it, ultimately, the work of social change. That's just part of it. The other part of it is in the eternity of the present, and doesn't have to do with evolutionary processes at all, but has to do with bringing us back to our original, true natures from whatever habit-molds that our perceptions, that our thinking and feeling get formed into. And bringing us back to original true mind, seeing the universe freshly in eternity, yet any moment.

GENESON: You would like to see poetry "grounded" essentially, rather than off in some metaphysical flight?

SNYDER: I would like to see *people* "grounded."

GENESON: In touch with their environment?

SNYDER: In touch with their own lives.

GENESON: With their bodies?

SNYDER: Yes. And let the poetry do what it wants from that. Get the people grounded and the poetry'll take care of itself.

GENESON: A problem that might be suggested is that, in terms of the popular mind, few people read Pound, few people read Bly. How does one propagate these ideas, then?

SNYDER: Few people read Pound, that's true. But Pound's power is in his role as an influence, for sure. More people read Bly, considerably more. And he also is an influence. The game is not to be measured in terms of popularity or readibility anyway. It has its effect several steps down the line—. The kind of poetry that we're talking about now has indirect effects, not direct effects if you want to talk about "masses," although I don't know if at this point we are talking about the "masses."

GENESON: Well, the popular sense of the value of poetry to a society.

SNYDER: I'm not sure that *value* is the same word as *function*. The *value* of poetry and the *function* of poetry in a society are two different things.

The value and function of poetry can be said in very few words. One side of it is *in-time,* the other is *out-of-time.* The in-time side of it is to tune us in to *mother* nature and *human* nature so that we live *in time,* in our societies in a way and on a path in which all things can come to fruition equally, and together in harmony. A path of beauty. And the out-of-time function of poetry is to return us to our own true original nature at this instant forever. And those two things happen, sometimes together, sometimes not, here and there and all over the world, and always have.

Now whether or not that particular pattern of processes has had any great or small effects on the major flow of human social evolution is not something I can say. And yet if you look at a society that *sings* and that *dances* as a regular thing, it's not that it has an effect on their life—it *is* their life. It is their life: the lore of the culture is carried in the songs. And so poetry *is* our life. It's not that poetry has an effect on it, or a function in it, or a value for it. It *is* our life as much as eating and speaking is our life. It's like asking, "Well, what's the function of eating? What's the value of speaking?"

GENESON: Walt Whitman says we need a more democratic America, a mythology of America. Some people today say that consensus is gone in America, and there can be no mythology of America. How can these ideas be reconciled?

SNYDER: There's a poem that Tu Fu wrote after the capital of China, Chang-an, fell to An Lu-shan, who was a rebel, and it looked as though the whole dynasty had been overthrown.

He wrote, "Though the nation is lost, the mountains and rivers remain." The mountains and rivers remain. That's the real country.

GENESON: Do you think Whitman was talking about that?

SNYDER: I don't know if he was talking about it or not. When he says there should be more democracy, I go along with that. We all see what more democracy means, too. It means that the Navajo should get their own nation, that Rosebud and Pine Ridge maybe should be a separate nation, that the Indians of Puget Sound have fishing rights, that trees and rocks should be able to vote in Congress, that whales should be able to vote—that's democracy.

GENESON: But who votes for them? How do they vote?

SNYDER: Well, Christopher Stone, in his essay "Should Trees Have Standing?" said legalistically it's very simple—the court appoints someone to be their representative. Like someone to be the spokesman for the yellow pine-black oak communities of Northern California and Southern Oregon. That's a possibility. Legally, this is not out of line: it would be analogous to the court appointing someone, a lawyer, to speak for a minor, or for the interests of a mentally retarded person, something like that.

Actually, that's not so interesting. We can see it has been one of the jobs of poetry to speak for these things, to carry their voice into the human realm. That it *is* in poetry and in song and in ritual and in certain kinds of dance drama that the nonhuman realms have been able to speak to the human society. There are large numbers of people who don't have an ear for that anymore, although once we all had an ear for it. So yes, the democracy can be extended and if it is it'll be a great employment for poets. I mean they'll be talking about CETA, and the federal government will be appointing poets to be spokesmen for the short grass prairies of Montana, and we'll all have seats in Congress. (*He laughs.*)

GENESON: But shouldn't the poet represent with his pen, and not be present in any center of power?

SNYDER: Oh, he has to get his poetry reading down there,

that's all. They say, you know, when the time comes for speeches, they're going to be voting on whether or not to adopt laws which will prohibit tuna fishermen from catching porpoises in their nets. Everyone has been consulted except the porpoises. At that point we call on the poet from the marine mammals. What do the porpoises feel about that? So he gets up and does his dance. (*Sustained laughter.*)

GENESON: Do you actually foresee this?

SNYDER: Well, I'm saying that that's what Whitman foresaw when he said we should be more democratic. If he was a true poet he couldn't have foreseen anything less than that.

GENESON: Do you read Whitman for this kind of message?

SNYDER: What I read Whitman for is for inspiration. He's inspiring. I love to read "The Song of the Open Road," or "By Blue Ontario's Shores," or "Passage to India"—I love to read 'em aloud, to a small audience. He's a good *communal* poet in that way. I don't know if you could read *The Four Quartets* in a social atmosphere that is quite so delightful. You could create an atmosphere in which there was a great expression of respect. But not that goofy *expansion* of things that Whitman accomplishes, with funny lines like "tender and junior Buddha."

GENESON: Ought all poetry be able to be read aloud? Or should some poetry be contemplative?

SNYDER: Even contemplative poetry can be read aloud. Witness Gregorian chants. Or Japanese or Chinese sutra chanting. That's contemplative poetry read aloud.

GENESON: You mentioned Whitman as a communal poet: Can a true communal poetry be possible?

SNYDER: It has been. It's been practiced much through time and is probably more the case rather than the exception. But it seems very hard to do now, right now. And it hasn't been customary in any literate, civilized tradition, as far as I can see, although it certainly is there in all of the oral traditions. An oral tradition *is* virtually a communal poetry.

GENESON: Why is it difficult now?

SNYDER: Because of the stress on individual names. And because the emphasis is on keeping a text pure.

GENESON: I'm thinking of poetry in the Communist world—they obviously have a didactic poetry, a poetry which speaks to the masses and which glorifies the masses. Is that poetry?

SNYDER: Could be. I mean, it's got a good subject matter to start with. Excellent subject matter.

GENESON: I was thinking of those people who would say that, by definition, a mass poetry cannot be good or great poetry.

SNYDER: You know, if I can write a poem in praise of planet earth, or in praise of the Douglas fir forests in Northern Washington, I don't see why I can't write a poem in praise of the masses of China. (*He laughs.*) Obviously it's possible.

GENESON: But don't you, as an individual poet, envision certain problems living in China?

SNYDER: Sure. I can also envision a lot of pleasure. I like getting together with other people and working. Wailing away on a job.

GENESON: But are you talking now about work, or about poetry?

SNYDER: I'm talking about *work*. I *love* getting together with a bunch of people and wailing away, building an earth dam, or peeling poles, or trucking gravel. (*Laughter.*)

GENESON: That I can see. But when it comes to poetic expression?

SNYDER: Well, that comes at night when you have a little saké to pass around and a little bonfire, and then you start singing. And that's where you make up a song about how many beautiful wheelbarrows we wheeled around today, and put in a few jokes about somebody.

GENESON: On a personal level: is the individual poet important? Does he need recognition?

SNYDER: Some do, some don't. I think for a lot of poets recognition from their peers is essentially what they need. You know, architects seldom get recognition from the public—the public doesn't see what's going on. An architect is pleased to have a fellow architect say, "I saw what you did there—that's

76

really something." That's what you need, for the most part. People who crave recognition beyond that I tend to suspect a little bit as wanting some food for their ego, which won't do them any good. Excessive recognition—it does no harm to have lots of money, to be sure. That's not entirely true. But maybe it doesn't do much harm to have lots of money. But *recognition* can really be detrimental to somebody who's interested in getting their work done and not in collecting their Karma Cookies at testimonial dinners.

GENESON: So things like poetry prizes and awards are—

SNYDER: They don't do any harm as long as they don't make you come to New York and have a dinner to get the prize. That's what's nice about the Pulitzer—they send a check in the mail. (*He laughs.*)

I'll tell you what I get off on. I get off on getting an occasional letter from somebody I've never met that says, "I know what you're doing in that poem"; that tells me that I've got it across. That's the only thing that really—that's what I call recognition. Those little signs that what I am trying to do in my craft on its more subtle levels is occasionally working.

GENESON: Do you like the idea of gatherings of poets? What Allen Ginsberg has in Boulder? Do you think it's valuable to either the students or the poets who are there?

SNYDER: I'm not against it in principle. But I don't like to go to things in the summertime because I have work to do here. I appreciate those gatherings in the right atmosphere, which is not too hectic or too disorderly. I would like to be able to go to gatherings like that where we all participated in the cooking and in the washing of the dishes, and were not served things cafeteria style: plastic, with little old ladies who cleaned up after us. I don't like to live that way. I like to be involved in the cooking and the cleanup, too. Ginsberg once put his finger on it really nicely after staying three days at Kent State. He said, "This is like an Old Folks Home here where everything is done for you. Except everybody's young." Now, I'm not knocking the academies now, I'm knocking the style of life on campuses. So, in other words, I don't like gatherings of poets on campuses. They're crummy. And I don't like staying up too many nights in a row, drinking too much and just talking.

GENESON: You mention drinking: I wanted to ask you if a person can get poetic material from either drinking or from drugs.

SNYDER: Sure you can. Anything that starts your head going, or releases a flow of feeling from within. Maybe that happens accidentally and naturally sometimes when you're a little stoned, or you've been drinking. But you would be getting into trouble if you had to go back to the booze or the grass—if you got to think that that was the way to do it. We'll say it may have been really the way to do it for several poets who have killed themselves with booze—it's also self-destructive.

—Like Lew [Welch]. Or like Jack Spicer. Alcohol did 'em in, finally. Alcohol did 'em in, and I don't believe that was the only way they could have been inspired. Even though they do call alcohol *spirits*.

GENESON: But does one actually write while on these?

SNYDER: I don't. I've had probably more than my share of psilocybin, peyote, et cetera. And I don't recall having ever written anything that was particularly useful to me while under the influence of any of those. Just think it through, feel it through. As a matter of fact, some experiences like that, triggered by psychedelics or via meditation or long walks in the mountains or sweat-baths or whatever, are a little bit too precious and too pure to just run off and write about right away. You do yourself and them a disservice if you try to put them in print. In other words, you're being a poetic journalist, you want to get the news *right now*. Which is equivalent to picking up the first beads you find scattered inside the entrance to the cave and running out with them, rather than having the patience to go in deeper and deeper into the cave and ignore those little gewgaws at the entrance. So this is something that some poets see and some poets don't see.

I'm saying that *certain* states of mind are too special even to put into poetry. And that you mess yourself up if you try to do that, if you try to exploit them for poetry.

GENESON: Related to the idea of the poet as either individually important or as anonymous: you at one point have written that the poet should not say, "I did it," but instead there should be a sense of "cool water." Does that tie in with the idea of whether you want to be remembered after your death—with anonymity?

SNYDER: I don't think we have any choice whether we're going to be remembered or not remembered. I think that's what happens.

GENESON: Yes. But Borges, for example, told me he doesn't want to be remembered, that it's just important that poetry goes on, that the pool of literature is increased, and that it doesn't matter who did the increasing.

SNYDER: As Nanao Sakaki, the great Japanese wandering poet, once said to me, "No need to survive." *"No need* to survive." (*The repetition is spoken as a hoary old man in robes would speak it.*) And that sums it all up. Absolutely. Not just poetry. Not the race. The whole universe. "No need to survive." It doesn't matter. To speak to anonymity: you can't really claim the poem is your own, so you'd feel dishonest if you took too much credit for it.

GENESON: Not your own because inspired?

SNYDER: Because inspired. Because from a place that your day-to-day mind isn't making happen. It's your original mind, which isn't mirrors—it belongs to everybody.

GENESON: *The* original mind?

SNYDER: *The* original mind. Original Mind is doing it, like it's doing everything else, too. And so you can't look at a poem—I mean literally you get a good poem and you don't know where it came from. "Did I say that?" And so all you feel is: you feel humility and you feel gratitude. And you'd feel a little uncomfortable, I think, if you capitalized too much on that without admitting at some point that you got it from the Muse, or whoever, wherever, or however. Which is just simply a confession that we're all part of everything. And if one individual seems to stand out, that's okay for that individual to stand out but that individual should remember, and we should all remember, that his standing out is only part of the dance, too.

GENESON: In your Introduction to *Selected Poems of Lew Welch* you mention that poets are the "sons of witches." Are you referring here specifically to the feminine self of the poet? Is this just a metaphor that you're using?

SNYDER: Well, it's an attempt to try to clarify what the language of Muses means, and also what is involved in the psychology of male poets. I don't know *what* applies in the psychology of female poets. I think that there is quite obviously an intense and deep connection between mother and son, and that the son relationship to the complex tooth-mother ecstatic-mother type is apt to produce environmentally, psychologically, genetically, by whatever means, the line of magic that produces poetry.

Let me expand on that. To be a poet you have to be tuned into some of the darkest and scariest sides of your own nature. And for a male, the darkest and scariest is the destructive side of the female.

GENESON: That's what you mean by the "tooth-mother"?

SNYDER: Right. As an infant in your dependence you trust, and in a sense *crave,* the female to be beneficent, because of the helplessness. The mother is, in general, the nourisher. But the female, as well as the male, also has a negative side. To a male child the negative side of the mother is the darkest, scariest thing he can perceive. What could be scarier than that? A bunch of scary warriors coming through would be rationally acceptable—they're not your mother, at least.

So a woman who, of her own nature, has a dark side—she will also be creative. Something is triggered by being a witness to that most paradoxical of human situations, witnessing the dark and the light side of the mother simultaneously. Most people only witness the light side of the mother. Literally. They only see the bright side of the mother, in one way or another. But some people see the *dark* side of the mother. If you only see the dark side you probably go crazy. The poet holds the dark and the light in mind, together. Which, by extension, means birth and death in its totality. We worship not only the positive forces, the life-giving forces—not just that. We can all say, "Ah, planet earth biosphere, mother earth, mother wonderful—all these green plants." But there's also death, there's also the unknown, there's also the demonic. And that's the womb and the tomb, that's samsara, that's birth and death, that's where the Buddhists go in. And that's where poetry goes in: That's where poetry gets its hands on something real. And it is triggered, I think—in many people I know it is triggered by seeing *that* in their infancy as a condition of the universe in the psychology of their own life.

GENESON: You suggest that just *poets* see that. Wouldn't there be people who, for example, would see the same thing as the poet and yet never write a line of poetry?

SNYDER: Sure.

GENESON: And is this related to the idea of the Muse as woman, unifying the dark and light?

SNYDER: The *paradox* is there. That which is born must die. The womb is the gate to the tomb—to put it in the sense that the ancients saw it. A very ancient perception.

GENESON: In your poem, "The Real Work," you mention that the "real work" is

> washing and sighing,
> sliding by.

What exactly is "the real work"?

SNYDER: I've used that phrase, "the real work," a few times before. I used that term, "the real work," and then I asked myself a lot: what is the real work? I think it's important, first of all, because it's good to work—I love work, work and play are one. And that all of us will come back again to hoe in the ground, or gather wild potato bulbs with digging sticks, or hand-adze a beam, or skin a pole, or scrape a hive—we're never going to get away from that. We've been living a dream that we're going to get away from it, that we won't have to do it again. Put that out of our minds. We'll always do that work. That work is always going to be there. It might be stapling papers, it might be typing in the office. But we're never going to get away from that work, on one level or another. So that's real. The real work is what we really do. And what our lives are. And if we can live the work we have to do, knowing that we are real, and it's real, and that the world is real, then it becomes right. And that's the *real work:* to make the world as real as it is, and to find ourselves as real as we are within it.

I used that phrase again at the end of the poem "I Went into the Maverick Bar," where we go back out of that bar in Farmington, New Mexico, out onto the highway

> under the tough old stars—
>
> . . .
>
> To the real work, to
> > "What is to be done."

To take the struggle on without the *least* hope of doing any good. To check the destruction of the interesting and necessary diversity of life on the planet so that the dance can go on a little better for a little longer. The other part of it is that it is always here,

> washing and sighing,
> sliding by.

That was the wash of the waves on the island out in San Francisco Bay with the seabirds, and the feeding and schooling of the little fish—that's going on. The *real work* is eating each other, I suppose.

GENESON: This is beginning to sound like the Auden quote— that poetry changes nothing.

SNYDER: Yes. Well, in that sense poetry does no more than woodchopping, or automobile repair, or anything else does because they're all equally real.

GENESON: Poetry does as much as?

SNYDER: As much as and no more than anything else. It's all real.

THE ZEN OF HUMANITY

The following statement was made in 1976 during a long and ambling panel discussion at Swarthmore College with Snyder, Philip Whalen, and Will Petersen. Snyder and Whalen had come to the campus to give a poetry reading; Petersen, an old friend and graphic artist, had mounted a retrospective show of his stoneprints in the McCabe library in conjunction with the reading and had come up from West Virginia to participate in the activities. It was a question of Petersen's that elicited Snyder's remarks, a query as to why Snyder stayed with Zen as primary.

I stay with Zen, because sitting, doing zazen, is a primary factor. Sitting is the act of looking-in. Meditation is fundamental, you can't subtract anything from that. It's so fundamental that it's been with us for forty or fifty thousand years in one form or another. It's not even something that is specifically Buddhist. It's as fundamental a human activity as taking naps is to wolves, or soaring in circles is to hawks and eagles. It's how you contact the basics and the base of yourself. And Zen has cut away a lot of frills, to keep that foremost.

Now the completion of this is understood very clearly in the Tibetan tradition when they speak of the three mysteries: body, speech, and mind. This is fundamental Buddhism to me; it's fundamental to existence itself, and Buddhism is about existence. The three things that are closest to us—our bodies, our minds, and our language—are the three things we know least about, that we pay least attention to, that we use as our tools throughout our lifetimes to various relatively limited ends, including survival, but there's very little attention to the fact of existence of this in its own right. A simple message of the teaching is that much of the pain, suffering, confusion, and contradiction you encounter in your own life is simply caused by not paying attention to what you have closest to you from the beginning and then using it well: body, speech, and mind. The three practices are, then: sitting meditation, for exploring the mind; singing or chanting, or poetry or mantras, for exploring speech and voice; and yoga, or dance, or hoeing the garden and gathering firewood, for the exploration of the body. We all do all these things, so all that needs to be added to that is a real awareness and attention in the doing, and a realization of the marvelousness, the mysteriousness, of all these simple acts, which again comes back to the sitting meditation, because it's at that point that you can really nurture and contact the marvelousness—and also the tiresomeness [in your life]. Trungpa makes a good point about how meditation is boring, and that how learning what boring is is very important. It's yourself that you're dealing with, not some kind of outside stimuli to keep you amused.

For myself personally all I would add to that are some very ancient and to me beautiful and useful ways of handling things: attention to place; gratitude to the physical universe and to all the other beings for what they exchange with you; good health, good luck, good crops. Basic old-style religion.

And, this is a Vajrayana point, proper attention to your dreams, fairy tales, and myths, as a kind of ancient universal, human psychological lore that you can and do contact. So koans, Aitken Roshi says, these meditations, poems or anecdotes or riddles, are the folklore of Zen, and we turn to that folklore again and again, and with the aid of a teacher reach out in ourselves and also benefit from much of the learning of others before us, the *sangha*.

And I turn that over one more way—I feel that mythology and folklore are the *koans* of humanity and that all of humanity has that as its store of feelings to deeply return to over and over again, and to make one more leap into a very sizable community.

TRACKING DOWN THE
NATURAL MAN

Colin Kowal is a carpenter; he lives and works in Snyder's home territory. Kowal conducted the following stand-up interview—Snyder was burning brushpiles throughout the questioning—for the Western Slopes Connection, *a local counterculture newspaper that was published in Nevada City, California, until early 1979.*

KOWAL: Your earlier books dealt with a lot of searching, the germinal ideas that still appear in your books. There was a sense of questioning, searching, actual physical traveling around, hitchhiking. Now, in *Turtle Island* it seems like you're proposing more answers than questions. Does this reflect an assuredness, a sense of being centered?

SNYDER: Well, maybe in some ways it does do that. It's certainly true that there's a lot of traveling and exploring, both physically and psychologically, in my earlier books. At the same time the earliest of them, *Riprap* and *Myths and Texts,* were not really my earlier poetry. They come after ten years of writing poetry. I did have a certain vision and focus established by the time I did *Myths and Texts,* which in some senses I've been following since. Maybe some of the solidity in *Turtle Island* is because of my sense of place, living here in Nevada County. I certainly feel good and strong about being in a place that I intend to live in for the rest of my life. I think that this is a basic human need. Which is not to say that a certain amount of traveling and wandering isn't also a need. But my earliest poems start here in America on the Pacific Coast, with travels in India and Japan in between. So it does complete a circle. Starting with Douglas fir and Ponderosa pine and ending with Douglas fir and Ponderosa pine.

KOWAL: My feeling is that we like to draw a lot of practical working knowledge from the Indians. But that we can't truly be Indians because we live in a highly technological society; there's too many of us here and not enough land to actually copy their lifestyle. I was wondering; what is the best thing that we can absorb from those peoples?

SNYDER: Well, the sense of "nativeness," of belonging to the place, to begin with, is critical and necessary. It doesn't matter what color your skin is, it's a matter of how you relate to the land. Some people act as though they were going to make a fast buck and move on. That's an invader's mentality. Some people are beginning to try to understand where they are, and what it would mean to live carefully and wisely, delicately in a place, in such a way that you can live there adequately and comfortably. Also, your children and grandchildren and generations a thousand years in the future will still be able to live there. That's thinking as though you were a native. Thinking in terms of the whole fabric of living and life. The Native American people lived fifty thousand years in California, perhaps.

In our present over-speeded and somewhat abnormal historical situation, the long stability of traditional peasant cultures or primitive hunting and gathering cultures seems maybe dull. That's the way modern Americans would look, say, at the Paiute, or even at Chinese peasants. Long, tiresome centuries, with nothing happening. But from the spiritual standpoint, the evolution of consciousness goes at a different pace. It's like zazen, like meditation. You sit for hours and nothing seems to be happening. I think maybe human spiritual evolution is similar to that. What looks like long dull centuries of simple cultures are intense meditations on one level in which inner discoveries are gradually being made. When we steer toward living harmoniously and righteously on the earth, we're also steering toward a condition of long-term stability in which the excitement, the glamour will not be in technology and changing fads. But it will be in a steady enactment and reenactment over and over again of basic psychological inner spiritual dramas, until we learn to find our way through to the next step. And that's why monasteries go on the way they do for centuries. And then they move just a little bit. One more thing.

I'm fascinated by that scale of time and by that scale of commitment, both to the land and to the process of evolution of consciousness. And I think the Indians have, thus, not only something to teach us about place and plants, and timber management, and game management, but also something to teach us about patience and long term commitment to a spiritual path.

KOWAL: Do you ever feel like you're a hopeless idealist?

SNYDER: No. Never. (*Laughter.*) I've always considered myself very practical.

KOWAL: What you're saying is perfectly practical and I'm sure there are a few people around who understand it. But the masses love technology. There's no way they're going to shut off the billboards on the other side of the Bay Bridge.

SNYDER: I love technology, too. But it's all a matter of scale. I've been reading *Ishi* again and he was a beautiful technician. Theodora Kroeber describes how he held the piece of obsidian and the deer antler that he pressed with, the steadiness and precision with which he shaped a head. Now that's beautiful technology, appropriate technology. It does just what he wants for him and the materials are easily available. So technology's not bad. We have to be masters of it, not have it master of us. And then we can enjoy it.

Knowing how to prune a fruit tree is technology. Knowing what cycle to plant a garden in is also, in a sense, technology. In other words, useful skills and useful tools are not in themselves wrong. But it's being tricked or dazzled by them that throws us off. Then we think we're less real than our tools.

We're so impressed by our civilization and what it's done, with our machines, that we have a difficult time recognizing that the biological world is infinitely more complex. And we have no understanding really of how it works. Yet in most people's minds, nature looks simple and man's technology looks wonderfully complicated and elaborate. Something to be very proud of. In fact, our most elaborate technology, say computers, is only the tiniest fraction of the brain of a mouse. They couldn't do what a mouse does.

KOWAL: People in your position are few, people who are artists who are surviving by their art, and who aren't involved so much in the ripoff. I would like to live off my poetry or songs, but it's not happening. So I'm roofing, contributing to the development of the country. On a pure way of looking at things, I'm doing a service. Putting shelter over peoples' heads. At the same time, I'm helping turn this place into that which I went away from. I came to the country for simple living, yet I have to survive. There's more construction now. I'm making it easier than ever before. Most people up here are in the same position. Living off arts and crafts is not for the many. Most people are living off the growing technology and development. How can it be switched around?

SNYDER: First of all, you must realize that these are abnormal times and there's no way that any of us can keep ourselves pure. We just have to keep as clear a head as possible and steer away from the worst of it. But everybody's involved in it. You can try in your personal lifestyle to do what is right. But making a living is to connect yourself with the economy. Some choices are better choices. And if you're lucky, you can be working as a carpenter on a school or a home for a friend. At another time, you might need money for land payments and you might have to go work in a subdivision. All that can be said is that we can balance that out by the work we do for the community on the positive side.

To get back to that point: Right Livelihood. Work that doesn't cheat people: logging, farming, crafts, skills, services, those are all valid. But we feel bad because we find ourselves doing things which are implicitly valid but are hooked up somehow to the economic growth system which is out of control. At least if you are aware of it, it helps.

KOWAL: There's almost an analogy there to what you eat. Whether you're eating vegetables, meat, or sand, you're involved in the ripoff.

SNYDER: I don't think eating is ripping off. We can't look at it that way.

KOWAL: Well, it does have that aspect.

SNYDER: No, because we're edible too.

KOWAL: But I'm not offering myself up to somebody as food.

SNYDER: You'd better. Sooner or later. If you look at life itself as a ripping off process, then your metaphysics are hopeless. Your only choice then is to reject the world and opt entirely for spirit. Which has meant historically to neglect the biological and to really rip off nature consequently. Like puritanism does. Opts entirely for spirit and in its capitalist version allows for total exploitation of nature because nature is not particularly important.

But you hit on a very sensitive thing, which is that relationship with food. If you think of eating and killing plants or animals to eat as an unfortunate quirk in the nature of the universe, then you cut yourself from connecting with the sacramental energy-exchange, evolutionary mutual-sharing aspect of life. And if we talk about evolution of consciousness, we also have to talk about evolution of bodies, which takes place by that sharing of energies, passing it back and forth, which is done by literally eating each other. And that's what communion is.

And that's what the shamanist world foresees. That's one of the healthiest things about the primitive worldview is that it's solved one of the critical problems of life and death. It understands how you relate to your food. You sing to it. You pray to it, and then you enjoy it.

KOWAL: Do you feel like most of your Dharma is with people here in the country or with your reading audience?

SNYDER: There are two kinds of human sets that we all relate to. One is our network and the other is our community. Some peoples don't have communities to relate to and only relate to the network. The network is like: all the dentists in the United States have a magazine and they have conferences and they all talk the same lingo and don't talk to anybody else. That's a network. There's a poet's network. And I correspond with poets all over the U.S. and other parts of the world. We have a lot in common—a lot of shoptalk with each other. There's a network of intellectuals, university professors, students, graduate students, ecological radicals, and so forth that I'm connected with. That gives me a certain sustenance and part of my work lies with that. Like the Ananda people connect with a Paramahansa Yogananda network all over the world.

But there's also the community, who are the people in the place that you live. The thing about a network is that everybody speaks the same language and more or less agrees with each other. The thing about a community is that you don't all agree with each other and there are problems that you have to live with and work out over a long scale of time. I find for my work and my own spiritual growth that the kind of life that happens in a community is, if anything, more valuable than that of the network. Because the network really does encourage you to think that you're important, but the community doesn't. I have followers, if you want to use the word, across the U.S. in the poetry and Zen Buddhist networks. I don't have followers on the San Juan Ridge because we all know each other too well. I haven't been such a big influence here—the two things I think every house should have, an entranceway where you can take off your boots and hang up your raincoat and a pantry where you can store your food—now, practically none of my friends who have built their houses up here have done that.

Poetry is not about lifestyle. And my Zen Dharma is not about lifestyle really. On a low level, lifestyle on a low level.

KOWAL: Oh, but it's still there.

SNYDER: But it's not much. Living your life is living your life.

KOWAL: Yes, but you'll say something like "walked out this morning and saw deer shit on the trail" and that'll turn somebody in the city onto a whole different lifestyle.

SNYDER: Or it completely leaves them cold. They don't give a shit about deer shit in the road.

KOWAL: Oh, I bet they do.

SNYDER: I know people who'd say, "Go out there in the woods? Are you kidding?" You need a broader reach than that. And poetry has to have a broader reach than that. The city is just as natural as the country, let's not forget it. There's nothing in the universe that's not natural by definition. One of the poems I like best in *Turtle Island* is "Night Herons," which is about the naturalness of San Francisco. Got to get rid of these dualisms.

KOWAL: Do you approach writing as a job?

SNYDER: Well, some kinds of writing like translations and essay writing I approach like I'm building a chicken coop. You get your materials laid out; you make your plans. And you go right ahead and do it. Writing poetry's not like that. Writing poetry is delicate and unpredictable and requires a continual openness to inner surprises and a willingness to pay attention to very subtle signs. If you don't notice them, you slide over them and miss the point.

KOWAL: Do you consider yourself to be a very open person? Sometimes I think of you as a very open person and sometimes very closed.

SNYDER: Open and closed is always a two-way thing. I'm open to people who approach with good manners and I'm closed to people who don't. People who don't realize that everybody has their own space and everybody is busy doing something. You have to go through certain steps and certain rituals in approaching somebody else's territory, just like two squirrels or two hawks. Americans are terrible that way.

I try to approach others carefully and to assess whether or not I'm welcome and whether or not they have the time to talk to me. And I would only ask the same of others.

THE *EAST WEST* INTERVIEW

Peter Barry Chowka interviewed Snyder in New York City over a five-day period in April of 1977. The interview was conducted in Allen Ginsberg's apartment, on the subway, while walking the New York City streets. Snyder was in New York to give a series of readings and to participate in a conference sponsored by the American Academy of Poets on "Chinese Poetry and the American Imagination."

Chowka is a free-lance writer and researcher whose detailed, indepth studies of subjects ranging from fast-food chains to the politics of cancer have been widely published. The interview first appeared in the summer, 1977, issues of East West Journal.

CHOWKA: You have said that you left graduate school "to pursue the Dharma which had become more interesting to me." In some detail, could you recount the context—influences, people, books—of those years which led you to Buddhism?

SNYDER: When I was young, I had an immediate, intuitive, deep sympathy with the natural world which was not taught me by anyone. In that sense, nature is my "guru" and life is my sadhana. That sense of the authenticity, completeness, and reality of the natural world itself made me aware even as a child of the contradictions that I could see going on around me in the state of Washington, in the way of exploitation, logging, development, pollution. I lived on the edge of logging country, and the trees were rolling by on the tops of trucks, just as they are still. My father was born and raised on the Kitsap County farm that my grandfather had homesteaded; he was a smart man, a very handy man, but he only knew about fifteen different trees and after that he was lost. I wanted more precision; I wanted to look deeper into the underbrush.

I perceived, also without it being taught to me, that there were such things as native people who were still around. In particular, one of them was an old man who came by about once a month to our little farm north of Seattle selling salmon that his people had smoked. They were Salish people who lived in a little Indian settlement on the shores of Puget Sound a few miles from us. My childhood perception of the world was white people, a few old Salish Indians, and this whole natural world that was half-intact and half-destroyed before my eyes.

At that age I had no idea of European culture or of politics. The realities were my mind, my self, and my place. My sympathies were entirely with my place—being able to see Mount Rainier far off to the east on a clear day or to climb the bluff of the hill to the west and look out over Puget Sound and the islands and see the Olympic Mountains. That was far more real to me than the city of Seattle, about ten miles south, which seemed like a ghost on the landscape.

(*Peter Orlovsky joins us at this point.*)

ORLOVSKY: What kind of a farm did your father have?

SNYDER: It was a little dairy farm, only two acres in pasture, surrounded by woods. As early as I was allowed, at age nine or ten, I went off and slept in the woods at night alone. I had a secret camp back in the woods that nobody knew about; I had hidden the trail to it. As soon as my father figured I knew how to put out a campfire, he let me go off and cook for myself and stay a day or two.

CHOWKA: This interest was mainly self-taught?

SNYDER: Very much self-taught. As soon as I was permitted, from the time I was thirteen, I went into the Cascade Mountains, the high country, and got into real wilderness. At that age I found very little in the civilized human realm that interested me. When I was eleven or twelve, I went into the Chinese room at the Seattle art museum and saw Chinese landscape paintings;

they blew my mind. My shock of recognition was very simple: "It looks just like the Cascades." The waterfalls, the pines, the clouds, the mist looked a lot like the northwest United States. The Chinese had an eye for the world that I saw as real. In the next room were the English and European landscapes, and they meant nothing. It was no great lesson except for an instantaneous, deep respect for something in Chinese culture that always stuck in my mind and that I would come back to again years later.

When I went into college I was bedeviled already by the question of these contradictions of living in and supposedly being a member of a society that was destroying its own ground. I felt the split between two realms that seemed equally real, leading me into a long process of political thought, analysis, and study, and—of course—the discovery of Marxist thought. For a long time I thought it was only capitalism that went wrong. Then I got into American Indian studies and at school majored predominantly in anthropology and got close to some American Indian elders. I began to perceive that maybe it was all of Western culture that was off the track and not just capitalism—that there were certain self-destructive tendencies in our cultural tradition. To simplify a long tale, I also saw that American Indian spiritual practice is very remote and extremely difficult to enter, even though in one sense right next door, because it is a practice one has to be born into. Its intent is not cosmopolitan. Its content, perhaps, is universal, but you must be a Hopi to follow the Hopi way.

By this time I was also studying Far Eastern culture at Reed College. I read Ezra Pound's and Arthur Waley's translations of Chinese poetry, a translation of the *Tao Te Ching,* and some texts of Confucius. Within a year or so I went through the *Upanishads, Vedas, Bhagavad-Gita,* and most of the classics of Chinese and Indian Buddhist literature. The convergence that I found really exciting was the Mahayana Buddhist wisdom-oriented line as it developed in China and assimilated the older Taoist tradition. It was that very precise cultural meeting that also coincided with the highest period of Chinese poetry—the early and middle T'ang Dynasty Zen masters and the poets who were their contemporaries and in many cases friends—that was fascinating. Then I learned that this tradition is still alive and well in Japan. That convinced me that I should go and study in Japan.

CHOWKA: How did you discover that it was still alive?

SNYDER: By reading books and also by writing letters. It's obvious that Buddhism presents itself as cosmopolitan and open to everyone, at least if male. I knew that Zen monasteries in Japan would be more open to me than the old Paiute or Shoshone Indians in eastern Oregon, because they *have* to be open—that's what Mahayana Buddhism is all about. At that point, spring 1952, I quit graduate school in linguistics and anthropology at Indiana University and hitchhiked back to Berkeley to enroll in the Oriental languages department at the University of California so I could prepare myself to go to Asia. I spent my summers working in the Northwest in lookouts and trail crews and logging and forest service jobs, like a migratory bird going north in summer and returning south in winter.

CHOWKA: You have said that you taught yourself zazen from books although you then decided a teacher was necessary.

SNYDER: I decided that quite clearly when I was twenty-one or twenty-two.

CHOWKA: And after that, then, you grounded yourself in the languages and philosophy to prepare to go to Japan?

SNYDER: Right, although sitting, you know, isn't that hard a thing to learn, if you understand what posture is.

ORLOVSKY: In what year did you first sit in meditation?

SNYDER: It must have been in '49 that I taught myself to sit.

CHOWKA: Is there a particular book which gave you the direction?

SNYDER: Several translations of various texts from India and China told how to sit. And looking at a good statue and seeing that it has good posture and how the legs are crossed—it's not hard. I soon corrected my errors because you cannot sustain sitting for very long if your posture is off; it becomes painful, breath doesn't feel right, et cetera.

ORLOVSKY: Did you sit regularly from '51 on?

SNYDER: Pretty much. Not a whole lot—though maybe a half an hour every morning when I was going to graduate school. When I was working in the mountains in the summers, I was able to sit a lot.

ORLOVSKY: By '55 was your sitting practice different from when you began?

SNYDER: I didn't feel self-conscious about it anymore. When I first sat, I recall how very strange, how very un-Western, it felt. I remember at Indiana University I was doing zazen in the apartment that I shared with the anthropologist Dell Hymes. Somebody walked in and caught me sitting there and I felt strange, they felt strange, and then it got all around the university: "That graduate student from Oregon does weird things." But that's the way it was, twenty years ago! It's nice now that people can sit cross-legged and nobody pays much attention.

ORLOVSKY: When did you first sit ten hours a day?

SNYDER: I never started sitting like that until I went to Japan and was forced to. I still wouldn't sit ten hours a day unless somebody forced me, because there's too much other work in the world to be done. Somebody's got to grow the tomatoes. There's not going to be that much meditation in the world if we're going to have a democratic world that isn't fueled with nuclear energy, because there isn't that much spare energy. We damn well better learn that our meditation is primarily going to be our work with our hands. We can't have twenty-five percent of the population going off and becoming monks at the expense of the rest, like in Tibet; that's a class structure thing, a by-product of exploitation—sitting an hour a day is not. Sitting ten hours a day means that somebody else is growing your food for you; for special shots, okay, but people can't do it for a whole lifetime without somebody else having to give up their meditation so that *you* can meditate.

CHOWKA: When you first began sitting, how did it change your life? Did it immediately affect the poetry you were writing, or was the effect more gradual?

SNYDER: It was gradual.

CHOWKA: But you knew when you began sitting that you liked it and wanted to continue it.

SNYDER: I had a pretty fair grasp of what the basic value of meditation is—an intellectual grasp, at least—even then. It wasn't alien to my respect for primitive people and animals, all of whom/which are capable of simply just *being* for long hours of time. I saw it in that light as a completely natural act. To the contrary, it's odd that we don't do it more, that we don't, simply like a cat, *be* there for a while, experiencing ourselves as whatever we are, without any extra thing added to that. I approached meditation on that level; I wasn't expecting anything to happen. I wasn't expecting instantaneous satori to hit me just because I got my legs right. I found it a good way to be. There are other ways to be taught about that state of mind than reading philosophical texts: the underlying tone in good Chinese poetry, or what is glimmering behind the surface in a Chinese Sung Dynasty landscape painting, or what's behind a haiku, is that same message about a way to *be,* that is not explicatable by philosophy. Zen meditation—zazen—is simply, literally, a way to be, and when you get up, you see if you can't be that way even when you're not sitting: just *be,* while you're doing other things. I got that much sense of sitting to make me feel that it was right and natural even though it seemed unnatural for a while.

CHOWKA: Could you tell us about your teacher, Oda Sesso?

SNYDER: I spent my first year in Japan living in Shokoku-ji, learning Japanese and serving as personal attendant to Miura Isshu Roshi. As my first teacher, he instructed me to continue my studies with Oda Sesso Roshi, who was the head abbot of Daitoku-ji at that time. So I went up to Daitoku-ji, was accepted as a disciple by Oda Sesso, and started going to sesshins and living periodically in the monastery.

I still think a lot about Oda Sesso Roshi. You know, we have an image of Zen masters: Rinzai masters are supposed to shout and hit you; Soto Zen masters are supposed to do something else—I'm not sure what. In actual fact, they're all very human and very different from one another. Oda Roshi was an especially gentle and quiet man—an extremely subtle man, by far the subtlest mind I've ever been in contact with, and a marvelous teacher whose teaching capacity I would never have recognized if I hadn't stayed with it, because it was only after five or six years that I began to realize that he had been teaching me all along. I guess that's what all the roshis are doing: teaching even when they're not "teaching." One of the reasons that you have to be very patient and very committed is that the way the transmission works is that you don't *see* how it works for a long time. It begins to come clear later. Oda Roshi delivered *teisho* lectures in so soft a voice nobody could hear him. Year after year, we would sit at lectures—lectures that only roshis can give, spontaneous commentaries on classical texts—and not hear what he was saying. Several years after Oda Roshi had died one of the head monks, with whom I became very close, said to me, "You know those lectures that Oda Roshi gave that we couldn't hear? I'm beginning to hear them now."[6]

CHOWKA: How did you come to choose Rinzai over Soto Zen, or was it a function of the contacts you had made?

SNYDER: It was partly a function of contacts. But if I'd had a choice I would have chosen Rinzai Zen. As William Butler Yeats says, "The fascination of what's difficult / has dried the sap out of my veins. . . ." The challenge of koan study—the warrior's path, almost—and maybe some inner need to do battle ("Dharma combat") were what drew me to it. By the time I went to Japan, I had the language capacity to handle the texts enough to be able to do it. Another reason: the koans are a mine of Chinese cultural information. Not only do they deal with fundamental riddles and knots of the psyche and ways of unraveling the Dharma, it's done in the elegant and pithy language of Chinese at its best, in which poetry (a couplet, a line, or even an entire poem) is employed often as part of the koan.

CHOWKA: You wrote in *Earth House Hold:* "Zen aims at freedom through practice of discipline," and the hardest discipline is "always following your own desires." Within that context, how is the "original mind" or "no mind" of Zen different from the so-called unenlightened normal consciousness of a non-Buddhist?

SNYDER: Unenlightened consciousness is very complicated—it's not simple. It's already overlaid with many washes of conditioning and opinion, likes and dislikes. In that sense, enlightened, original mind is just simpler, like the old image of the mirror without any dust on it, which in some ways is useful. My own personal discovery in the Zen monastery in Kyoto was that even with the extraordinary uniformity of behavior, practice, dress, gesture, every movement from dawn till dark, in a Zen monastery everybody was really quite different. In America everybody dresses and looks as though they are all different, but maybe inside they're all really the same. In the Far East, everybody dresses and looks the same, but I suspect inside they're all different. The dialectic of Rinzai Zen practice is that you live a totally ruled life, but when you go into the sanzen room, you have absolute freedom. The roshi wouldn't say this, but if you forced him to, he might say, "You think our life is too rigid? You have complete freedom here. Express yourself. What have you got to show me? Show me your freedom!" This really puts you on the line—"Okay, I've *got* my freedom; what do I want to do with it?" That's part of how koan practice works.

CHOWKA: Why did you not take formal vows of a monk?

SNYDER: Well, I actually did at one time; my hair is long now simply because I haven't shaved it lately. There is no role for a monk in the U.S.

CHOWKA: While you were studying in Japan for most of ten years, you always knew that you'd return to the U.S.?

SNYDER: Oh, yes.

CHOWKA: Was your return hastened by the death of your teacher?

SNYDER: Probably. At a certain point I realized that, for the time, I'd been in Japan enough. I began to feel the need to put my shoulder to the wheel on this continent. It wasn't just returning—the next step of my own practice was to be here.

CHOWKA: When you were interviewed in 1967 for *Conversations: Christian and Buddhist* you were studying at Daitoku-ji but not actually living in the monastery.

SNYDER: I was living in a small house that was ten minutes' walk from the monastery. It was really necessary to spend most of the time at the house, because in a monastery you have no access to texts or dictionaries. All of the other monks had already memorized everything, literally. As an outsider-novice-foreigner, you are continually wrestling with problems of translation and terminology—you have to go look things up.

ORLOVSKY: Was there a library at the monastery?

SNYDER: No. There are no books and no reading at a monastery. There was also the economic consideration of having to make a living. So part-time I taught conversational English to the engineers of various electronics companies to make enough money to rent a little house, buy my food, ride a bicycle.

CHOWKA: A decade ago, or even earlier, you prophesied a great development of interest in Buddhism in the West. In 1967 you said, "The 'truth' in Buddhism is not dependent in any sense on Indian or Chinese culture." Could you comment on your view now that ten years have passed?

SNYDER: What I felt at the time and what I think all of us feel is that we're talking about the Dharma without any particular cultural trapping. If a teaching comes from a given place, it's a matter of courtesy and also necessity to accept it in the form that it's brought. Things take forms of their own; we don't *know* what's going to happen in the future. The Buddhadharma, which is the Dharma as taught by a line of enlightened human beings (rather than the Dharma as received from deities via trance, revelation, or *bhakta,* which is what Hinduism is) is *nirmanakaya*-oriented—it goes by changeable bodies. Right now it goes primarily through human bodies. Already it is all over the globe, and it has no name and needs no name.

CHOWKA: In a 1961 essay, "Buddhist Anarchism," revised in *Earth House Hold* as "Buddhism and the Coming Revolution," you criticize institutional Buddhism in the East as "conspicuously ready to accept or ignore the inequalities/tyrannies of whatever political system it found itself under." In your 1967 conversation with Aelred Graham in Kyoto, you spoke of the other organized faiths as "degenerations that come with complex civilized social systems," although you added that "In the Christian world there is much more serious thought about the modern age and what to do with it than in the Buddhist world." Now, ten years later, Buddhism, especially the Tibetan and Zen varieties, is much more widely available in North America. Has the coming of the Buddhadharma to the West altered your view about its complicity with degenerate, oppressive political systems?

SNYDER: Not particularly. It has to be understood that in Asia—India, China, and Japan—the overwhelming fact of life for three millennia has been the existence of large, centralized, powerful states. Much as in Europe until the Renaissance, it was assumed that the government was a reflection of natural order and that if there were inequalities or tyrannies that came from the government, although one might dislike them, there was no more use in complaining about them than there would be use in complaining about a typhoon. The better part was to *accept.* One of the most interesting things that has ever happened in the world was the Western discovery that history is arbitrary and that societies are human, and not divine, or natural, creations—that we actually have the capacity of making choices in regard to our social systems. This is a discovery that came to Asia only in this century. We in the West have an older history of dealing with it.

The organizations of Buddhism, Taoism, and Hinduism made the essential compromises they had to make to be tolerated by something that was far more powerful than themselves, especially in the imperial state of China. One of those compromises was to not criticize the state. You can't blame them for it, because they had no sense of there being an alternative. Even so, an interesting set of historical moves occurred in Chinese Buddhism. During the early period of Zen an essay was written that said Buddhist monks do not have to bow to the emperor since they are outside the concerns of the state. Later, in the thirteenth century, in Zen monasteries, sutras were chanted on behalf of the long life of the emperor; the monasteries supported and aided the regime. What it came to most strikingly was the almost complete cooperation of the Buddhist establishment in Japan (with some notable exceptions) with the military effort of World War II.

We don't have to go into how passionately nationalistic the Hindu Party of India is. The fact is that all of the world religions—Hindu, Buddhist, Islamic, Christian—share certain characteristics because they are all underneath the umbrella of civilization. As it turns out, one of the "World Religions'" main functions is to more or less support or reinforce the societies they are within. Even those who define their mission as liberating human beings from illusion have found it necessary to make compromises so that their little subculture wouldn't lose its tax-free buildings and landholdings and would be permitted to have a corner of existence in the society. This is also why monastic institutions are celibate. If they gave birth to their own children, they would become a tribe; as a tribe, they would have a deeper investment in the transformation of society and would *really* be a thorn in the flesh. As it is, if they simply are replenished by getting, in every generation, individuals from outside, they will never have that much investment in social transformation. If it's not a celibate *sangha,* then it's an alternative to society, an alternative that might be too threatening.

CHOWKA: You wrote in *Earth House Hold:* "Beware of anything that promises freedom or enlightenment—traps for eager and clever fools—three-quarters of philosophy and literature is the talk of people trying to convince themselves that they really like the cage they were tricked into entering." In an interview in the August *East West Journal,* Robert Bly agrees with Gurdjieff, who said it is important that true teachings be somewhat hard to find—there is only so much "knowledge" available at any one time and one's psyche can be changed only if a lot of knowledge comes at once; if offered to too many people via mass movements, the knowledge is dissipated. Bly goes on to say that there has been an infantilization of humanity, citing a book on the subject by Kline and Jonas, whose thesis is that each generation following the Industrial Revolution is more infantile than the previous, thus, for example, needing many more supportive devices merely to survive.

Would you comment on these observations in terms of your own view of the spiritual movements which have proliferated during this decade?

SNYDER: There is a very fine spiritual line that has to be walked between being unquestioning/passive on the one hand and obnoxiously individualistic/ultimately-trusting-no-one's-ideas-but-your-own on the other. I don't think it's uniquely American; I think that all people have these problems on one level or another. Maybe that's one meaning of the Middle Way: to walk right down the center of that. In one of the Theravada scriptures the Buddha says, "Be a light unto yourself. In this six-foot-long body is birth and death and the key to the liberation from birth and death." There is one side of Buddhism that clearly throws it back on the individual—each person's own work, practice, and life. Nobody else can do it for you; the Buddha is only the teacher.

Americans have a supermarket of adulterated ideas available to them, thinned out and sweetened, just like their food. They don't have the apparatus for critical discernment either. So that the term "infantilization" is something I can relate to. I think there's a lot of truth in it. The primary quality of that truth is the lack of self-reliance, personal hardiness—self-sufficiency. This lack can also be described as the alienation people experience in their lives and work. If there is any one thing that's unhealthy in America, it's that it is a whole civilization trying to get out of work—the young, especially, get caught in that. There is a triple alienation when you try to avoid work: first, you're trying to get outside energy sources/resources to do it for you; second, you no longer know what your own body can do, where your food or water come from; third, you lose the capacity to discover the unity of mind and body via your work.

The overwhelming problem of Americans following the spiritual path is that they are doing it with their heads and not with their bodies. Even if they're doing it with their heads *and* bodies, their heads and bodies are in a nice supportive situation where the food is brought in on a tray. The next step, doing their own janitorial work and growing their own food, is missing, except in a few places.

CHOWKA: Would you like to comment on those few places where people are provided with teaching which requires work, too?

SNYDER: The San Francisco Zen Center is a good example. In both the mountain and city centers they are striving conscientiously to find meaningful work for everybody—work that, in the city center, is not foppish or artificial but is relevant to the immediate needs of that neighborhood, which is predominantly black, with lots of crime. Zen Center opened a grocery store and a bakery; they sell vegetables from their garden in Green Gulch in the grocery store. It's an effort in the right direction—that which is "spiritual" and that which is sweeping the floor are not so separated. This is one of the legacies of Zen, Soto or Rinzai—to steadily pursue the unity of daily life and spiritual practice.

CHOWKA: Does that relate to a difference between the Chinese and Indian legacies as they've been applied to North American spiritual disciplines?

SNYDER: The spiritual legacy of Chinese culture is essentially Zen or Ch'an Buddhism. The secondary spiritual legacy of China is in the aesthetics—the poetry and painting (Confucius, Lao-tzu, and Chuang-tzu are included in that; also Mencius, whose work will be appreciated more in time for its great human sanity, although it's deliberately modest in its spiritual claims). Ch'an Buddhism added to Indian Buddhism the requirement that everybody work: "a day without work, a day without food." The cultural attitude toward begging in China was totally different from that in India; the Chinese public wouldn't stand for beggars. Long before, in India, giving money to beggars was considered praiseworthy and merit-creating, which created an ecological reinforcing niche for people to live by begging. You can see it in the strictly yogic or sadhu approach, which separates lay society from people who follow a religious path. When the society is so strictly split, lay people have no access to spirituality except to gain merit by giving money to those who follow a spiritual path. This is true today in Theravadin countries like Thailand and Ceylon.

In India, although the word bhikkhu means beggar, it also meant that these people were aristocrats; they wou'dn't pick up a hoe, they certainly wouldn't touch shit, they wouldn't even touch money, because that's demeaning and low-caste. This is a tendency that possibly is imbibed from Brahminism and caste structure. So although Buddhism starts out with no caste, with the concept of bhikkhu, nonetheless, the bhikkhu becomes rated so highly socially that, in a certain way, he's like a Brahmin—he's "pure" and shouldn't become defiled in any way. This lays the groundwork for the later extraordinary hierarchization of the Buddhist orders of India and Tibet. The Chinese culture wouldn't tolerate that. Po-chang, in his monastic rules written during the T'ang Dynasty, makes clear that begging is not a main part of our way of self-support. Our way of self-support is to grow our own food, build our own buildings, and make everybody, including the teacher, work. As long as he's physically able, the teacher must go out and labor with his hands along with his students. For all of the later elegance and elitism that crept into Ch'an and Zen, this is a custom that has not broken down. Roshis in Japan do physical work alongside their monks, still. That has been for them a source of abiding health.

There are other things within the Ch'an administrative structures, within the monasteries, which are quite amazingly democratic when it comes to certain kinds of choices. All of the monks—whether novices or elders—have an equal vote. That is a Chinese quality in that spiritual legacy. Another development that is Chinese, as far as I can tell, is group meditation. In India and Tibet, meditation is practiced primarily in a solitary form. The Chinese and Japanese made group sitting a major part of their practice. There is a communalization of practice in China, a de-emphasis of individual, goofy, yogic wandering around. For the Chinese monk there is a phase of wandering, but it's after many years of group practice/labor. I love both India and China; I love the contradictions. I can identify with both—see the beauty of both ways of going at it.[7]

CHOWKA: Buddhism as practiced in the East is criticized often for being dominated by males. Is this situation improving?

SNYDER: The single most revolutionary aspect of Buddhist practice in the United States is the fact that women are participating in it. This is the one vast sociological shift in the entire history of Buddhism. From the beginning, women essentially had been excluded. But in America, fully fifty percent of the followers everywhere are women. What that will do to some of these inherited teaching methods and attitudes is going to be quite interesting.

One of the things I learned from being in Japan and have come to understand with age is the importance of a healthy family. The family is the Practice Hall. I have a certain resistance to artificially created territories to do practice in, when we don't realize how much territory for practice we have right at hand always.

CHOWKA: In the later draft of your essay "Buddhist Anarchism" you added the qualifier "gentle" to the "violence" you felt was occasionally permissible in dealing with the system. I'm curious if this word change means your view was tempered during the eight years that separated the two versions; perhaps oddly, too, the adjective "gentle" appeared at the end of the sixties, when talking about "violence," at least, had become quite acceptable.

SNYDER: If I were to write it now, I would use far greater caution. I probably wouldn't use the word "violence" at all. I would say now that the time comes when you set yourself against something, rather than flow with it; that's also called for. The very use of the word "violence" has implications—we know what they are. I was trying to say that, to be true to Mahayana, you have to act in the world. To act responsibly in the world doesn't mean that you always stand back and let things happen: you play an active part, which means making choices, running risks, and karmically dirtying your hands to some extent. That's what the Bodhisattva ideal is all about.

CHOWKA: You once mentioned an intuitive feeling that hunting might be the origin of zazen or samadhi.

SNYDER: I understand even more clearly now than when I wrote that, that our earlier ways of self-support, our earlier traditions of life prior to agriculture, required literally thousands of years of great attention and awareness, and long hours of stillness. An anthropologist, William Laughlin, has written a useful article on hunting as education for children. His first point is to ask why primitive hunters didn't have better tools than they did. The bow of the American Indians didn't draw more than forty pounds; it looked like a toy. The technology was really very simple—piddling! They did lots of other things extremely well, like building houses forty feet in diameter, raising big totem poles, making very fine boats. Why, then, does there seem to be a weakness in their hunting technology? The answer is simple: they didn't hunt with tools, they hunted with their minds. They did things—learning an animal's behavior—that rendered elaborate tools unnecessary.

You learn animal behavior by becoming an acute observer—by entering the mind—of animals. That's why in rituals and ceremonies that are found throughout the world from ancient times, the key component of the ceremony is animal *miming*. The miming is a spontaneous expression of the capacity of becoming physically and psychically one with the animal, showing the people know just what the animal does. (*Snyder mimics a lizard.*) Even more interesting: in a hunting and gathering society you learn the landscape as a field, multidimensionally, rather than as a straight line. We Americans go everywhere on a road; we have points A and B to get from here to there. Whenever we want something, we define it as being at the end of this or that line. In Neolithic village society, that was already becoming the case, with villages linked by lines. In a society in which everything comes from the field, however, the landscape with all its wrinkles and dimensions is memorized.

You know that over there is milkweed from which come glue and string, over the hill beyond that is where the antelopes water. . . . That's a field sensing of the world. All of it partakes of the quality of samadhi.

More precisely, certain kinds of hunting are an entering into the movement-consciousness-mind-presence of animals. As the Indians say, "Hunt for the animal that comes to you." When I was a boy I saw old Wishram Indians spearing salmon on the Columbia River, standing on a little plank out over a rushing waterfall. They could stand motionless for twenty to thirty minutes with a spear in their hands and suddenly—they'd have a salmon. That kind of patience!

I am speculating simply on what are the biophysical, evolutionary roots of meditation and of spiritual practice. We know a lot more about it than people think. We know that the practices of fasting and going off into solitude—stillness—as part of the shaman's training are universal. All of these possibilities undoubtedly have been exploited for tens of thousands of years—have been a part of the way people learned what they are doing.

CHOWKA: In a 1975 interview you said, "The danger *and* hope politically is that Western civilization has reached the end of its ecological rope. Right now there is the potential for the growth of a real people's consciousness." In *Turtle Island* you identify the "nub of the problem" as "how to flip over, as in jujitsu, the magnificent growth-energy of modern civilization into a nonacquisitive search for deeper knowledge of self and nature." You hint that "the 'revolution of consciousness' [can] be won not by guns but by seizing key images, myths, archetypes . . . so that life won't seem worth living unless one is on the transforming energy's side." What specific suggestions and encouragement can you offer today so that this "jujitsu flip" can be hastened, practically, by individuals?

SNYDER: It cannot even be begun without the first of the steps on the Eightfold Path, namely Right View. I'll tell you how I came to hold Right View in this regard, in a really useful way. I'm a fairly practical and handy person; I was brought up on a farm where we learned how to figure things out and fix them. During the first year or two that I was at Daitoku-ji Sodo, out back working in the garden, helping put in a little firewood, or firing up the bath, I noticed a number of times little improvements that could be made. Ultimately I ventured to suggest to the head monks some labor- and time-saving techniques. They were tolerant of me for a while. Finally, one day one of them took me aside and said, "We don't want to do things any better or any faster, because that's not the point—the point is that you live the whole life. If we speed up the work in the garden, you'll just have to spend that much more time sitting in the zendo, and your legs will hurt more." It's all one meditation. The importance is in the right balance, and not how to save time in one place or another. I've turned that insight over and over ever since.

What it comes down to simply is this: If what the Hindus, the Buddhists, the Shoshone, the Hopi, the Christians are suggesting is true, then all of industrial/technological civilization is really on the wrong track, because its drive and energy are purely mechanical and self-serving—*real* values are someplace else. The real values are within nature, family, mind, and into liberation. Implicit are the possibilities of a way of living and being which is dialectically harmonious and complexly simple, because that's the Way. Right Practice, then, is doing the details. And how do we make the choices in our national economic policy that take into account *that* kind of cost accounting—that ask, "What is the natural-spiritual price we pay for this particular piece of affluence, comfort, pleasure, or labor saving?" "Spiritual price" means the time at home, time with your family, time that you can meditate, the difference between what comes to your body and mind by walking a mile as against driving (plus the cost of the gas). There's an accounting that no one has figured out how to do.

The only hope for a society ultimately hell-bent on self-destructive growth is not to deny growth as a mode of being, but to translate it to another level, another dimension. The literalness of that other dimension is indeed going to have to be taught to us by some of these other ways. There are these wonderfully pure, straightforward, simple, Amish, won't-have-anything-to-do-with-the-government, plain folk schools of spiritual practice that are already in our own background.

The change can be hastened, but there are preconditions to doing that which I recognize more clearly now. Nobody can move from Right View to Right Occupation in a vacuum as a solitary individual with any ease at all. The three treasures are Buddha, Dharma, and Sangha. In a way the one that we pay least attention to and have least understanding of is Sangha—community. What have to be built are community networks—not necessarily communes or anything fancy. When people, in a very modest way, are able to define a certain unity of being together, a commitment to staying together for a while, they can begin to correct their use of energy and find a way to be mutually employed. And this, of course, brings a commitment to the place, which means right relation to nature.

CHOWKA: In a letter to the editor in a recent issue of *East West Journal,* a reader wondered if the editor and other people who share so-called "new consciousness" occupations (jobs that might be more independent and rewarding, or less alienating than the norm), in interacting primarily with other like-minded or similarly engaged people, tend to become isolated from ordinary mainstream humanity. In talking with Aelred Graham ten years ago, you touched on this: "I almost can't escape from a society of turned-on people, which amounts to ten or fifteen thousand. . . . This is my drawback . . . I never meet those people (bourgeois, puritanical) in America." In his *Southern Review* article on your work in 1968, Thomas Parkinson notes (although he does not agree with) one criticism of your writing, thus: "Snyder does not face problems of modern life. . . . His poetry doesn't answer to the tensions of modern life and depends on a life no longer accessible or even desirable for man." There is also the danger that Herbert Marcuse sees in *One Dimensional Man,* that "the peculiar strength of the technological culture [is] to be able to make tame commodities out of potentially revolutionary states of consciousness." Would you comment on these points—isolation, irrelevance, and cooptation?

SNYDER: Taking the first point: At the time I talked to Graham, I was living in Kyoto and I hadn't lived in America in any serious way for many years; that was a very special statement I made to Graham at that point. In actual fact, I've lived more in the flux of society on more levels than practically anybody I know. I've held employment on all levels of society. I can pride myself on the fact that I worked nine months on a tanker at sea and nobody once ever guessed I had been to college.

I grew up with a sense of identification with the working class. I have lots of experience with this society—always have had and still do. I realize the danger of getting locked into a self-justifying group, which we see all around us. Since I've come back to the U.S.—and for the last seven years I've lived in rural California—I've been able to live and move with all kinds of people, which has been very good for me. A lot of my friends are doing the same. The whole "back to the land" movement, at least in California, at first had the quality of people going off into little enclaves. But the enclaves broke down rapidly as people discovered not only that they would *have to* but that they would *enjoy* interacting with their backwoods neighbors. A wonderful exchange of information and pleasure came out of what originally was hostile; each side discovered that they had something to learn from the other. Certain things that at first were taboo have become understood and acceptable.

The interesting point is the criticism of my poetry as invoking essentially outmoded values or situations that are not relevant or desirable. It's complicated to try to defend that. The answer lies in a critique of contemporary society and the clarification of lots of misunderstandings people have about what "primitive" constitutes, and even simpler clarifications about what your grandmother's life was like. It isn't really a main thrust in my argument or anyone else's I know that we should go backward. Whenever you get into this kind of discussion, one of the first things you are charged with from some corner is that

111

"Well, you want to go backwards." So you have to answer it over and over again, but still people keep raising it. I remember a journalist once told David Brower of Friends of the Earth, "You want us to go back to the Stone Age!" and David replied, "Well, I'd be quite content to go back to the twenties, when the population was half of what it is now." Jerry Brown asked me the same question in a discussion about three weeks ago; he said, "You're going against the grain of things all the time, aren't you?" I said, "It's only a temporary turbulence I'm setting myself against. I'm in line with the big flow." (*Snyder laughs.*)

When we talk about a "norm" or a "Dharma," we're talking about the grain of things in the larger picture. Living close to earth, living more simply, living more responsibly, are all quite literally in the grain of things. It's coming back to us one way or another, like it or not—when the excessive energy supplies are gone. I will stress, and keep stressing, these things, because one of the messages I feel I have to convey—not as a preaching but as a demonstration hidden within poetry—is of deeper harmonies and deeper simplicities, which are essentially sanities, even though they appear irrelevant, impossible, behind us, ahead of us, or right now. "Right now" is an illusion, too.

The point by Marcuse that you raised is a real danger. I'm conscious enough of it, but I'm not sure about how one handles it except by being really careful and wary; that's one of the reasons why I stay out of the media pretty much—maybe a simpleminded way of keeping myself from being preempted or made into a commodity.

CHOWKA: You studied anthropology in school and it's remained one of your main interests. Some time ago you said, "We won't be white men 1,000 years from now . . . or fifty years from now. Our whole culture is going someplace else." More recently, you told a Montana newspaper, "We may be the slight degeneration of what was really a fine form," as you cited a recent study of a Stone Age habitation in southern France which showed the people to have had larger brains, much leisure time, and an aesthetic or religious orientation. Would you give your anthropologically grounded innate/intuitive assessment in this larger "Dharma" view of where we're at now?

SNYDER: We have to develop a much larger perspective on the historical human experience. Much of that perspective is simply knowing the facts—facts that are available but simply haven't entered into people's thinking. This is the new, larger humanism, and it helps us to understand our spiritual strivings, too. On the average, the human brain was larger 40,000 years ago than it is now. Even the Neanderthal had a brain larger than modern man. This information is from a study of skull casts. Whether or not it's terribly relevant, we don't know, but it's a very interesting point. Marshall Sahlins, an economic anthropologist at the University of Chicago, in *Stone Age Economics,* offers the research, methodology, and conclusion that upper Paleolithic people worked about fifteen hours a week and devoted the rest of their time to cultural activities. That period and shortly thereafter coincides with the emergence of the great cave art—for example, in the Pyrenees in southern France. We can only speculate about who those people were; however, we do know that they were fully intelligent, that their physical appearance was no different from people you see today (except their stature—at least that of the Cro-Magnon—was a little larger), and that they ate extremely well.

Not only are there thousands of caves and thousands of paintings in the caves, but paintings occur in caves two miles deep where you have to crawl through pools of cold water and traverse narrow passages in the dark, which open up on chambers that have great paintings in them. This is one of our primary koans: What have human beings been up to? The cave tradition of painting, which runs from 35,000 to 10,000 years ago, is the world's longest single art tradition. It completely overwhelms anything else. In that perspective, civilization is like a tiny thing that occurs very late.

The point that many contemporary anthropologists, like Sahlins and Stanley Diamond, are making is that our human experience and all our cultures have not been formed within a context of civilization in cities or large numbers of people. Our

113

self—biophysically, biopsychically, as an animal of great complexity—was already well formed and shaped by the experience of bands of people living in relatively small populations in a world in which there was lots of company: other life forms, such as whales, birds, animals. We can judge from the paintings, from the beauty and accuracy of the drawings, and also from the little Magdalenian stone carvings, the existence of a tremendous interest, exchange, and sympathy between people and animals. The most accurate animal drawings that have been done until modern scientific animal drawings are these cave drawings: right perspective, right attention.

To come a step farther: in certain areas of the world, the Neolithic period was long a stable part of human experience. It represented 8,000 to 10,000 years of relative affluence, stability, a high degree of democracy, equality of men and women—a period during which all of our vegetables and animals were domesticated, and weaving and ceramics came into being. Most of the arts that civilization is founded on, the crafts and skills, are the legacy of the Neolithic. You might say that the groundwork for all the contemporary spiritual disciplines was well done by then. The world body of myth and folklore—the motifs of folklore and the main myths and myth themes distributed universally around the globe—is evidence of the depth of the tradition. So, in that perspective, civilization is new, writing is even newer, and writing as something that has an influence on many people's lives came only during the last three or four centuries. Libraries and academies are very recent developments, and world religions—Buddhism among them—are quite new. Behind them are millennia of human beings sharpening, developing, and getting to know themselves.[8]

The last eighty years have been like an explosion. Several billion barrels of oil have been burned up. The rate of population growth, resource extraction, destruction of species, is unparalleled. We live in a totally anomalous time. It's actually quite impossible to make any generalizations about history, the past or the future, human nature, or anything else, on the basis of our present experience. It stands outside of the mainstream.

It's an anomaly. People say, "We've got to be realistic, we have to talk about the way things *are.*" But the way things for now *are* aren't real. It's a temporary situation.

CHOWKA: In *Earth House Hold* you wrote of Native Americans, "Their period of greatest weakness is over."

SNYDER: I hope that wasn't wishful thinking.

CHOWKA: You're not sure now?

SNYDER: Ah, it's touch and go. In a sense, they're in the same boat with all of us. Maybe a few of the peoples can hold something together because they have a population of sufficient size. But it's going to be very tricky. Diamond says the major theme of civilization is the slow but steady destruction or absorption of local, kin-based, or tribal populations by the Metropole. That process is still at work. The other side of it is the amazing resistance that some cultures show to being worn away, like the Hopi and the other Pueblos. They're incredibly strong and may well survive.

I've often wondered what makes these societies so tough. And it may well be that they are close to an original source of integrity and health. Erasing all negative associations for the word "primitive," it means *primus* or "first," like "original mind," original human society, original way of being. Another curious thing about the relationship between "primitive" and "civilized" is that no primitive society ever became civilized of its own free will; if it had the choice, it stayed itself.

In India today, three or four miles as the crow flies away from a 3,000-year-old agricultural civilization using Sanskrit, having temples and Brahmins—three miles up into the hills are original tribal societies that have lived that close to civilization for 3,000 years, and still they are the same people; they just can't be bothered. There is a reason why some of them are really strong; it's a systems/ecology reason, which I hit on finally after reading Margalef's book *Perspectives in Ecological Theory* and Eugene Odum.

Every given natural region has a potential top situation where all of the plants that will grow there have grown up now and all of those that will push out something else have pushed out something else, and it reaches a point of stability. If you cut all the forests and you wait many hundreds of years, it'll come to something again.

CHOWKA: It's an optimum condition.

SNYDER: This condition, called "climax," is an optimum condition of diversity—optimum stability. When a system reaches climax, it levels out for centuries or millennia. By virtue of its diversity it has the capacity to absorb all sorts of impacts. Insects, fungi, weather conditions come and go; it's the opposite of monoculture. If you plant a forest back into all white pine, one of these days the white pine blister rust comes along and kills all the white pine. If you have a natural mixed forest, the white pine will be hit a little by blister rust but they won't be in a solid stand, they'll be broken up. Another aspect of a climax situation is that almost half of the energy that flows in the system does not come from annual growth, it comes from the recycling of dead growth. In a brand-new system—for instance, after a piece of ground has been scraped with a bulldozer, when weeds and grass come up—the annual energy production is all new growth production; there is very little to be recycled. But with a forty percent recycling situation, there is a rich population of fungi, and beetles, and birds that feed on bugs, and predators that feed on birds that feed on bugs that eat the rotten wood; you've then achieved the maximum optimal biomass (actual quantity of living beings) in one place. This is also what is called "maturity." By some oddity in the language it's also what we call a virgin forest, although it's actually very experienced, wise, and mature. Margalef, a Spanish ecologist, theoretician, genius, has suggested that the evolution of species flows in line with the tendency of systems to reach climax. Many species exist in relation to the possibility of climax and to its reinforcement.

Certain human societies have demonstrated the capacity to become mature in the same way. Once they have achieved maturity, they are almost indestructible. But this kind of maturity has nothing to do with the maturity of civilization. (The only societies that are mature are primitive societies—they actually are that old, too: 30,000 years here, 10,000 years there.) "Civilization" is analogous to a piece of scraped-back ground that is kept perpetually scraped back so that you always get a lot of grass quickly every year—monoculture, rapid production, a few species, lots of energy produced, but no recycling to fall back on. So, civilization is a new kind of system rather than an old or mature one.

CHOWKA: An essay in *Turtle Island* tells us to "Find your place on the planet and dig in." Could you speak about your attempt to "dig in" in northern California, and the local political action you have found to be necessary?

SNYDER: To say "we must dig in" or "here we must draw our line" is a far more universal application than growing your own food or living in the country. One of the key problems in American society now, it seems to me, is people's lack of commitment to any given place—which, again, is totally unnatural and outside of history.

Neighborhoods are allowed to deteriorate, landscapes are allowed to be strip-mined, because there is nobody who will live there and take responsibility; they'll just move on. The reconstruction of a people and of a life in the United States depends in part on people, neighborhood by neighborhood, county by county, deciding to stick it out and make it work where they are, rather than flee. Zen Center has certainly demonstrated this with their tenacity in San Francisco, where, instead of being overwhelmed by the deterioration processes at work around them, they've reversed the flow by refusing to leave and by, against all odds, putting in a park—turning things around just by being there. Any group of people (not just Zen Center) who have that consciousness can do that. A corollary to that is my own experience in rural California: I have never learned so much about politics or been so involved in day-to-day social problems. I've spent years arguing the dialectic, but it's another thing to go to supervisors' meetings and deal with the establishment, to be right in the middle of whatever is happening right here, rather than waiting for a theoretical alternative government to come along.

I'll say this real clearly, because it seems that it has to be said over and over again: There is no place to flee to in the U.S. There is no "country" that you can go and lay back in. There is no quiet place in the woods where you can take it easy and be a stoned-out hippie. The surveyors are there with their orange plastic tape, the bulldozers are down the road warming up their engines, the real estate developers have got it all on the wall with pins on it, the county supervisors are in the back room drinking coffee with the real estate subdividers, the sheriff's department is figuring to get a new deputy for your area soon, and the forest service is just about to let out a big logging contract to some company. That's the way it is everywhere, right up to the north slope of Alaska, all through Canada, too. It's the final gold rush mentality. The rush right now is on for the last of the resources that are left standing. And that means that the impact is hitting the so-called country and wilderness. In that sense, we're on the front lines. I perceived that when I wrote the poem; that's why I called it "Front Lines." I also figured that we were going to have to stay and hold the line for our place.

A friend of mine came to where I live five years ago, and he could see what was going to come down. He said, "I'm not going to settle here, I'm going to British Columbia." So with his wife and baby he drove two hundred and fifty miles north of Vancouver, B.C., and then seventy miles on a dirt road to the end of the road, and then walked two miles to a cabin that they knew about, and bought a piece of land only a few miles south of the St. Elias range. That summer there they discovered they were surrounded by chain saws that were clear-cutting the forest, and that there were giant off-the-road logging trucks running up and down the seventy miles of dirt road, so that it was to take your life in your hands to try to go into town to get something. "Town" was a cluster of laundromats, discarded oil drums, and mobile homes that had been flown in. That's the world. My friends came back down to California; it was too industrial up there.

I would take this all the way back down to what it means to

get inside your belly and cross your legs and sit—to sit down on the ground of your mind, of your original nature, your place, your people's history. Right Action, then, means sweeping the garden. To quote my teacher, Oda Sesso: "In Zen there are only two things: you sit, and you sweep the garden. It doesn't matter how big the garden is." That is not a new discovery; it's what people have been trying to do for a long time. That's why there are such beautiful little farms in the hills of Italy, people did that.

CHOWKA: Could you give examples of some issues that have arisen in your county and that you've addressed—the kinds of action required and support you received?

SNYDER: One issue was building codes: housing and toilets. A number of people had their houses tagged as illegal, because they hadn't gotten a building permit, the construction used did not conform to the code, or they substituted outhouses for septic tanks.

CHOWKA: This happened where you live. What is it like there?

SNYDER: Genuinely rural and remote. A lot of time and work on the part of hundreds of people all over California, ultimately, went into fighting a tactic whose purpose was to try to get them out as an undesirable minority population who had moved in and lowered real estate values. Such things were reversed by intelligence and research, and the very clear argument that it's obviously unfair to impose suburban housing development standards in a rural area. Now some changes have been made in the code of California to permit rural people to build their homes in a simpler way. A small victory—to have an outhouse! Some other changes have been made in the code to make it legal not to have electricity and legal to have a wood stove. The codes were actually getting to the point where you *had* to have electricity to be legal. It's a small issue but one in which people's lives and homes are at stake.

More interesting is the question of schools, school boards, and the degree of autonomy you can practice with education if you have a school board with some kind of vision and a unity of purpose behind it. We went through quite a number building a public school locally—it was clearly the will of the people to build it in a beautiful, careful, and craftly way, not making it into an interchangeable-pod schoolhouse. Because the architects, Zach Stewart and Dan Osborne, who were hired by the school board also were visionary men with great patience, it was possible, at the cost of two extra years of work, to get the state to approve it. It was also possible because hundreds of people donated thousands of hours of free time to the building of it; it became a work of art. That's what a community can do for its children. It's also possible to keep on top of the local forest service and their timber policies in a way that the conservationists in the big city can't. They can do a lot—they have lobbyists with a lot of clout in Washington. But there are certain things that are effectively accomplished when local people say, "We don't like the way this is being handled here on public land." If you have both local people and people with a lobbyist in Washington coming with the same message, then you have something working on these public land managers, who tend to be rather arrogant.

Where I live, the greater proportion of the land in the county is public land; we find ourselves in the position of being the only ombudsman for the use of that land. Nobody else is watching but us. At the same time we can't be too unrealistic or idealistic about it, because we know what those jobs mean to our neighbors. If you want to say that there should be no more logging in this section, you also have to ask what the alternative employment will be. Many people where I live are interested in developing crafts, skills, industries, co-ops that give the whole population a long-range economic viability. So throughout California—which is my main area of experience—I know of both rural and urban enclaves that are trying to develop, on every level, appropriate technologies, both material and spiritual. And I guess it's going on all over the country.

* * *

CHOWKA: I wonder about the value given to poetry in our society. *Turtle Island,* which won for you a Pulitzer Prize and is by contemporary standards a successful poetry book (selling almost 70,000 copies), when compared to mass market novels, for example, has sold very little.

SNYDER: For a book of formal poetry, *Turtle Island* sold quite a bit. But it's only one kind of poetry. Actually, Americans love poetry, pay huge sums of money for it, and listen to it constantly. Of course, I'm talking about song, because poetry is really song. Rock 'n' roll, ballad, and all other forms of song are really part of the sphere that, since ancient times, has been what poetry is. If you accept poetry as song, then there are plenty of songs already which are doing most of the work that poetry is supposed to do for people.

CHOWKA: You're using song a lot more now in your own poetry, as in "California Water Plan."

SNYDER: Yes, I'm using literal song-voice, singing voice or chanting voice, in poetry and probably will be doing it more. But even the way I read the other poems has the element of song in it, because the intensification of language and the compression of the already existing sound-system musicality of the spoken language itself is manifested by the reading of the poem. Part of the work of the poet is to intensify and clarify the existing musical sound-possibilities in the spoken language.

CHOWKA: You speak a lot about the "old ways" and the fact that song comes from a prehistoric tradition. Is the fact that song is so popular today, in poetry and popular song, proof that these "old ways" cannot be lost, that they are with us still?

SNYDER: One of the things that little children do first is to sing and chant to themselves. People spontaneously sing out of themselves—a different use of voice. By "song" we don't have to limit ourselves to the idea of lyric and melody, but should understand it as a joyous, rhythmic, outpouring voice, the voice *as* voice, which is the Sanskrit goddess Vak—goddess of speech, music, language, and intelligence. Voice itself is a manifestation of our inner being.

CHOWKA: We know that poetry shares its roots with religion, music, dance. Why isn't poetry as compromised or diluted as you've said these other things—religion, music, et cetera—tend to be?

SNYDER: None of them is functioning with the wholeness that we can guess that they had once. That wholeness, in part, was a function of the fact that they all worked together: poetry didn't exist apart from song, song didn't exist apart from dance, dance didn't exist apart from ritual, ritual didn't exist apart from vision and meditation. Nonetheless, all of these forms have their own intrinsic validity. I wouldn't say that poetry today is any more valid than dance or drama.

CHOWKA: But you did say that in *Earth House Hold*.

SNYDER: Okay, I did say that, didn't I? What I meant was that poetry has maintained itself with more of its original simplicity perhaps than some of these other forms—it has taken on less technology in support of it. But then I would have to qualify that as to allow how the music which is popular song—which I think is a fascinating phenomenon apart from the fact that it's being used as a commodity—as it stands now is backed by a very complex technology; however, you can remove most of that technology and go back to an acoustic situation and it still has the power in a live setting.

CHOWKA: In *Earth House Hold* you write that "there comes a time when the poet must choose" between the "traditional-great-sane-ordered stream" and one that's "beyond the bound onto the way out, into . . . possible madness . . . possible enlightened return." Did you have yourself in mind when writing that? It's not completely clear if you've chosen one way or the other—I can see elements of both in your work.

SNYDER: I wrote that a long time ago, and I was able to say it because I could see both sides in myself and say, maybe somewhat artificially, that you have to be one way or the other. I'll rephrase it in terms of how I see it now: We have a sense that great artists and geniuses have to be crazy, or that genius and creativity are functions somehow of a certain kind of brilliant craziness, alienation, disorder, disassociation.

122

CHOWKA: Like Baudelaire, Rimbaud.

SNYDER: The model of a romantic, self-destructive, crazy genius that they and others provide us is understandable as part of the alienation of people from the cancerous and explosive growth of Western nations during the last one hundred and fifty years. Zen and Chinese poetry demonstrate that a truly creative person is more truly sane; that this romantic view of crazy genius is just another reflection of the craziness of our times. In a utopian, hoped-for, postrevolutionary world, obviously, poets are not going to have to be crazy and everybody, if they like, can get along with their parents; that would be the way it is. So I aspire to and admire a sanity from which, as in a climax ecosystem, one has spare energy to go on to even more challenging—which is to say more spiritual and more deeply physical—things. Which is not to disallow the fact that crazy, goofy, clowning, backwards behavior isn't fun and useful. In mature primitive societies the irrational goofy element is there and well accounted for.

CHOWKA: I want to return to this idea later in discussing the fifties. But first, who are some of the people you feel personify the "beyond the bound onto the way out" tradition today?

SNYDER: I don't know if I want to say anybody personifies it.

CHOWKA: You didn't have individuals in mind when you wrote it?

SNYDER: I can think of parts of individuals. I would say that maybe we can discriminate between poets who have fed on a certain kind of destructiveness for their creative glow (and some of those are no longer with us, consequently) as against those who have "composted" themselves and turned part of themselves back in on themselves to become richer and stronger, like Wendell Berry, whose poetry lacks glamour but is really full of nutrients.

CHOWKA: You mention Berry frequently; I gather he's one of your favorite poets. Could you talk about some other contemporary poets whom you read and enjoy?

SNYDER: I have a special regard for Robert Duncan because of his composting techniques and also because of his care, scholarship, acquaintance with the Western tradition and its lore, knowledge, and wisdom (which I have neglected)—I'm glad that he's doing it and I can learn from him. I'm glad that Robert Bly is looking at the Western tradition. I'm also a close reader of Michael McClure's poetry, for his long, careful, intense dedication to developing a specific biological/wild/unconscious/fairytale/new/scientific/imagination form. Maybe he's closer to Blake than anybody else writing. I can think of poets who are little known—like Robert Sund, who has only one book out—who have cultivated a fine observation and ear and tuned it to daily life, work, people, scenes of the West or wherever they are, who are unpretentious in the presentation of themselves, but who have very high-quality work. Wendell Berry is a man who does very high-quality work and is also a working farmer and a working thinker, who draws on the best of American roots and traditional mindfulness, like his Kentucky farming forebears, to teach us something that we're not going to learn by studying Oriental texts.

CHOWKA: He's grounded himself in this country.

SNYDER: He's grounded here, but at the same time opening it out so that we can say, "There was something like the Oriental wisdom here all along, wasn't there?"

CHOWKA: That wisdom tradition is universal.

SNYDER: It is universal, as good farming, and attention to how to treat things, are universal.

CHOWKA: The poets you've mentioned so far are all personal acquaintances to some degree. How much does knowing a poet personally, knowing how he/she writes, affect your appreciation of the poet's work?

SNYDER: I've run into poems by poets I haven't known in the least that have excited me instantaneously, like Lillian Robinson, who lives in upstate New York, whose work (a poem called "In the Night Kitchen") I saw in a little magazine. (I got her address and asked her to send me a couple more poems.) I watch for those things—for the growth of people who are our peers and contemporaries—and hopefully, too, I try to see something of what's coming in from other places.

124

I've been responding to your question about who I read and what I think of poets; I've been answering in a conventional modern American poet mold. I'd like to explain how I *really* do things, because it's part of my view and my practice. I no longer feel the necessity to identify myself as a member of the whole society.

CHOWKA: North American society?

SNYDER: Yes. It's too large and too populous to have any reasonable hope of keeping your fingers on it, except by the obviously artificial mode of mass media television, which I don't see anyway, and which presents only a very highly specialized surface from that society. What I realistically aspire to do is to keep up with and stimulate what I think is really strong and creative in my own viable region, my actual nation: northern California/southern Oregon, which we might call Kuksu country, subdivision of Turtle Island continent. Within that, I do know what's happening and I do read and follow and go to readings with and read poems with the poets who are beginning to develop a depth and a grounding out of it. We also have our own way of keeping touch in terms of our local drainage (which is the North Pacific) across the North Pacific rim, with companion poets in Japan, like Nanao Sakaki and his circle—great Japanese bioregional poets who, analogously to us calling North America "Turtle Island," call Japan "Jomonia" and have an island-Pacific-bioregion sense of it. I don't see anything provincial or parochial in it because it implies a stimulus to others to locate themselves equally well. Having done so, we will see a mosaic of natural regions which then can talk across the boundaries and share specifics with each other. Southwest specifics, like I get from the rancher-writer Drummond Hadley, teach me ecosystems and mind-understandings that are different from ours in the sense of how you relate to the blue sky and to turquoise. I can talk about how we relate to heavy winter rains and large conifers.

CHOWKA: But you retain still a global consciousness to the extent that you've identified nuclear power as the greatest danger to the planet, which is not purely a local issue.

125

SNYDER: There are two kinds of earth consciousness: one is called global, the other we call planetary. The two are 180 degrees apart from each other, although on the surface they appear similar. "Global consciousness" is world-engineering-technocratic-utopian-centralization men in business suits who play world games in systems theory; they include the environmentalists who are employed at the backdoor of the Trilateral Commission. "Planetary thinking" is decentralist, seeks biological rather than technological solutions, and finds its teachers for its alternative possibilities as much in the transmitted skills of natural peoples of Papua and the headwaters of the Amazon as in the libraries of the high Occidental civilizations. It's useful to make this distinction between a planetary and a global mind. "Planetary mind" is old-ways internationalism which recognizes the possibility of one earth with all of its diversity; "global consciousness" ultimately would impose a not-so-benevolent technocracy on everything via a centralized system.

CHOWKA: I'd like to return the discussion to your career, and how you began to have your work published. At one point you said that very early you decided, in effect, that "there was nothing more to be done vis-à-vis seeking a poetic career." Did publishing your first poems and books require some exertion or did it literally all fall into place without any effort?

SNYDER: I had sent poems around a little bit for a while. I think maybe only one or two things were published. It was partly a Buddhist decision. I was working for the forest, fixing trails up in the high country of Yosemite, I was getting more into meditation—walking or mountain meditation—by myself. I finished off the trail crew season and went on a long mountain meditation walk for ten days across some wilderness. During that process—thinking about things and my life—I just dropped poetry. I don't want to sound precious, but in some sense I did drop it. Then I started writing poems that were better. From that time forward I always looked on the poems I wrote as gifts that were not essential to my life; if I never wrote another one, it wouldn't be a great tragedy. Ever since, every poem I've written has been like a surprise. I've never expected or counted on

126

writing another one. What I really got to work on at that time was studying Chinese and preparing myself to go to Japan and study. But I guess I really didn't give up poetry enough because while I was in Japan I was always what is described as the lowest type of Zen student—the type who concerns himself once in a while with literature. So, I confess I did go on writing poems from time to time, which is inexcusable! I couldn't help myself.

CHOWKA: You mentioned China positively in *Turtle Island* ("I lost my remaining doubts about China") and in a letter about Suwa-no-se Island ("People's China has many inspiring examples"). You also published a poem in *The Back Country* titled "To the Chinese Comrades." What are your feelings about China now?

SNYDER: I guess I probably spoke too soon in saying I've lost my remaining doubts; I still have doubts about China—certainly doubts about China as a model for the rest of the industrial world. Many lessons, though, can be learned but they cannot be applied wholesale—people wouldn't stand for it. But, yes, China is filled with inspiring examples of cooperation, reforestation, and less inspiring examples like the campaign to kill sparrows some years ago.

CHOWKA: What about their disaffiliation with their spiritual lineage?

SNYDER: That doesn't trouble me too much. I believe the Chinese had been pretty well disaffiliated from that already for some time. But, in a sense, the primary values already had sunk in so deeply that they didn't have to articulate them much anymore. Also, as a student of Chinese history, I perceive a little about the cycles that it moves in. If the rest of the world holds together, I would bet that a century and a half from now China again will be deeply back into meditation, as part of the pendulum swing of things. In a way, People's China is a manifestation of wonderful qualities of cooperation and selfless endeavor toward a common goal that were there all along. The negative side, though, is that China has been the most centralized, bureaucratic, civilized culture on earth for the longest time; unquestionably because of that, much was lost within and without.

Much diversity was lost. The Chinese in the past, and probably still, don't have an appreciation for the ethnic or the primitive. For centuries, they have been looking down on their own border people or on the small aboriginal enclaves—tiny cultures in the hills of which there are still hundreds within China. So I feel ambivalent about China. Without doubt one can recognize the greatness of its achievement on all levels and think of it as a model of what a civilization can be; but then I can just as soon say, "But I wish there *weren't* any civilization!"

Sir Joseph Needham is very impressed by the Chinese revolution; in his book *Science and Civilization in China* he says that Taoism foreshadows the Revolution, and that's true. Taoism is a Neolithic world view and a matrilineal, if not matriarchal, Chinese world view that somehow went through the sound barrier of early civilization and came out the other side halfway intact, and continued to be the underlying theme of Chinese culture all through history up until modern times—antifeudalistic; appreciative of the female principle, women's powers, intuition, nature, spontaneity, and freedom. So Needham says that Taoism through history has been a 2,000-year-long holding action for China to arrive at socialism. That's how positively *he* looks at it. The contemporary Chinese look back on Taoism as a heritage in their past that as socialists they can respond to. Buddhism is a foreign religion—it came from India! But the Taoist component in Chinese culture will surely return again to the surface.

(*Peter Orlovsky enters the conversation.*)

ORLOVSKY: Are there any tribes in China still that have been left alone?

SNYDER: There are some. You can't communalize certain kinds of production in certain areas—you can't improve on what they're doing already. If a group has a good communal village agriculture—a hill situation not susceptible to use of tractors—it might as well be left alone.

The present Chinese regime, like every regime in the world, has been guilty of some very harsh and ethnocentric treatment of people, especially the Tibetans, which is inexcusable. At the

128

same time they hold out a certain measure of hope, especially to people of the Third World underdeveloped countries, who are offered only two models of what to do. One model is to plug into the nearest fossil fuel source and become a satellite country of the United States or some other industrial nation; the other option is the Chinese: get the landlords off your back, straighten out the tax structure, and then do better agriculture with the tools you have available. The Chinese are perhaps on the verge of becoming more industrialized, and this good opinion of them may soon evaporate; as a strategy for what they consider to be their own survival, they may go the same route we have. The other point I want to make is that although it's true that China is the world's most centralized and bureaucratic, the oldest, and in some ways the most autocratic civilization, at the same time it has been filled with a rich mix of humanity from north to south, east to west: dialects, subcultures, of all sorts, of great vigor—many of them in one way or another amazingly still around. But it isn't something we would want to be, we would never want to be as populated as China.

CHOWKA: One of the more interesting points to arise during the "Chinese Poetry and the American Imagination" conference this week is a question that you raised. We had assumed that there was a tone of intimacy, of cooperation, of communality in a lot of the Chinese poetry that was discussed. You wondered if the new, wider, Occidental interest in classical Chinese poetry presaged the development of similar qualities here.

SNYDER: I think it's inevitable that American society move farther and farther away from certain kinds of extreme individualism, for no reason other than that the frontier is gone and the population has grown; partially, it may be the social dynamics of crowding. (Although, of course, many societies that are not crowded are nonetheless highly cooperative.) But I didn't raise this point as a prophecy, but as a question. The negative side of the spirit of individualism—the "everybody get their own" exploitative side—certainly is no longer appropriate. It can be said to have been in some ways productive when there were enormous quantities of resources available; but it's counterproductive in a postfrontier society. It's counterproductive when the important insight for everyone is how to interact appropriately and understand the reciprocity of things, which is the actual model of life on earth—a reciprocal, rather than a competitive, network. The ecological and anthropological sciences are in the forefront of making models for our new value systems and philosophies. We are moving away from social Darwinism. As the evolutionary model dominated nineteenth- and early twentieth-century thinking, henceforth the ecological model will dominate our model of how the world is—reciprocal and interacting rather than competitive.

* * *

CHOWKA: Many of the ideas you've expressed are certainly as radical as those of Allen Ginsberg and the other writers who were part of the Beat literary group. You share a similar, unequivocal vision of where and how society went wrong, which unsettles many people. Compared to Allen and the others, however, relatively little has been written about you in a negative way. Why the difference?

SNYDER: Allen became extremely famous! He got a lot of negative criticism, but he also got an enormous amount of positive criticism. The proof of the pudding is in the eating: he sold hundreds of thousands of copies of *Howl*. It's great not to have had much negative criticism, but there are some people who never have had a negative word said about them, and nobody's read their books either. The point is to enter the dialogue of the times. Certainly, some of the things I have to say strike at the root. Until recently, most people, including Marxists, have been unable to bring themselves to think of the natural world as part of the dialectic of exploitation; they have been human-centered —drawing the line at exploitation of the working class. My small contribution to radical dialectic is to extend it to animals, plants: indeed, to the whole of life.

CHOWKA: I'd like to talk about your work in Governor Jerry

130

Brown's administration as a member of the Arts Council. What does that job entail?

SNYDER: As a member of the Arts Council, I attend monthly meetings and committee meetings, answer a lot of mail, talk to many people and check things out, so to speak, all of which is connected with some policies and ideas that we as a council of nine members are beginning to formulate on the thorny question of how to use the people's money—how to feed it back to the people for the support of art and culture.

CHOWKA: Are the members of the Council working artists?

SNYDER: With one exception they are all working artists, which was Brown's idea.

CHOWKA: The Council is new under his administration?

SNYDER: Yes. It's a departure from the usual arts commission being peopled by essentially wealthy patrons of the arts for whom being on a state's arts council is a social plum—perpetuating the idea that there are "good people" who have made a lot of money and also love the arts who then decide how to give money to artists. It was Brown's idea to change that, which has made a small ripple across the country; it demonstrates that artists can read, write, administer, and do things that a lot of people said they couldn't. (It takes me away from my own work, though.)

CHOWKA: When I met Robert Bly this week he told me he has strong objections to your being on the Arts Council; he sees a danger in the state trying to deal with and fund the arts in a centralized way.

SNYDER: This is a dialogue that goes on now across the U.S., in England, and in other places where the state uses public money to support art. When Governor Brown first took office, he had strong reservations about whether there should be a state arts council at all, from several standpoints, ranging from the question of "Is this a proper use of tax money?" to whether government involvement in the arts would result in implicit censorship or ultimately thought or aesthetic control. Those of us he talked to at that time shared those fears and worries, and were ourselves ambivalent about being on an arts council. But, it was with a strong experimental hope that there might be a way to use people's money to benefit creativity, avoiding these pitfalls, that we got involved.

There is no question that art meets real needs of the people. For artists—whether full-time professionals or part-time amateurs—ecologically, economically, their niche is there. But within the complexities of our present industrialized, civilized world, you have to come to grips with the problem in a new way. An economic subsidy of a very special order accounts for so much of the energy, affluence, craziness, and speed of the last eighty years. Fossil fuel subsidy is underwriting mass production. Fossil fuel energy is a subsidy from nature; we do not have to pay for the BTUs in oil what we would have to pay if it were not already concentrated and available in an easily usable form in the ground. Put simply, the arts—with the exception of certain modern media arts—are labor-intensive. Labor-intensive activities of any sort cannot compete with fossil-fueled ones—hand-thrown as against mass-produced pots, for example. As it happens, art cannot mass produce. To produce an opera requires hours of rehearsal; there is no way of automating that.

CHOWKA: And study, too—the preparation of an individual artist.

SNYDER: Yes. If we value art and higher cultural forms (and they should be valued, because they are preserves of the human spirit—as Lévi-Strauss says, "national parks of the mind"), then the people themselves are going to have to keep them going, until the time when the fossil fuel subsidy is withdrawn and the arts can compete in the free market economy like the family farm (when labor-intensive agriculture can be economically competitive once again). My view is that public support is necessary to carry the arts through, in the same way that we are trying to carry endangered species through.

Since we have taken on this task, we in California have been considered populists, because we have tried to adjust the balances of where money goes and what deserves support. We've put a stress on thinking of art in terms of creativity and process rather than commodity and product. We look on creativity as a birthright of everybody; we're trying to play down the sense of artist as special genius or talent, and be more sensitive to the community roles and possibilities of artists working on many levels of professionalism.

The local craftsperson or artist down the street is as valuable in being the yeast of social change and direction as anyone else. In terms of quality, we in California are concerned with recognizing and rewarding excellence, but we don't want to impose standards of excellence that derive simply from the Western European high cultural tradition. So our Arts Council is a very diverse group.

You raised the question of centralization. Actually, the Arts Council is less centralized than it would appear. The actual selection of who gets grants is decided by panelists—other artists or teachers—chosen from around the state who donate time to read applications. We translate their opinions into actions. Further, the state is divided demographically into five areas of racial, cultural, and economic spread, so that without compromising quality we make a point of affirmative action. We make sure that folks from the back country and the inner city know what's happening so that they can participate.[9]

CHOWKA: You don't see any conflict between having a state job administering money to artists and writers and being a poet and writer yourself?

SNYDER: Arts Council members don't get paid. The time I give to it is public service time; and it takes a lot of my time. You have to trust that the people whom the governor appoints are going to be fair. The fact that we're artists should be seen as a plus, because we're in a position to know from inside with our own hearts how things can and should be. The knowledge of what kind of work it takes to be an artist is also one of our strengths. Concerning other conflicts of interest, we members of the Arts Council are the only artists in the state who cannot apply for grants!

CHOWKA: Can you say more about your own evolving practice?

SNYDER: You're asking me what is my Buddhist practice? I'll ask you, "What do you mean by 'practice'?"

CHOWKA: The realization that there is something to be done.

SNYDER: What about the realization that there is nothing to be done?

CHOWKA: Then why would one go to Japan to study?

SNYDER: But what is "practice"?

CHOWKA: Sitting, for one thing.

SNYDER: Sitting—okay. So you're defining "practice" essentially as a concrete, periodic activity.

CHOWKA: Partially.

SNYDER: It might be mantra chanting, too; it might be doing a certain number of prostrations everyday.

Periodic, repetitive behavior, to create, recreate, enforce, reinforce certain tendencies, certain potentialities, in the bio-psyche. There is another kind of practice which also is habitual and periodic, but not necessarily as easily or clearly directed by the will: that's the practice of necessity. We are six-foot-long vertebrates, standing on our hind legs, who have to breathe so many breaths per minute, eat so many BTUs of plant-transformed solar energy per hour, et cetera. I wouldn't like to separate our mindfulness into two categories, one of which is your forty-minute daily ritual, which is "practice," and the other not practice. Practice simply is one intensification of what is natural and around us all of the time. Practice is to life as poetry is to spoken language. So as poetry is the practice of language, "practice" is the practice of life. But from the enlightened standpoint, all of language is poetry, all of life is practice. At any time when the attention is there fully, then all of the Bodhisattva's acts are being done.

I've had many teachers who have taught me good practices, good habits. One of the first practices I learned is that when you're working with another person on a two-person crosscut saw, you never push, you only pull; my father taught me that when I was eight. Another practice I learned early was safety: where to put your feet when you split wood so that the ax won't glance off and hurt your feet. We all have to learn to change oil on time or we burn out our engines. We all have to learn how to cook. By trial and error, but also by attention, it gets better. Another great teaching that I had came from some older men, all of whom were practitioners of a little-known esoteric indigenous Occidental school of mystical practice called mountaineering. It has its own rituals and initiations, which can be very severe. The intention of mountaineering is very detached—it's not necessarily to get to the top of a mountain or to be a solitary star. Mountaineering is done with team work. Part of its joy and delight is in working with two other people on a rope, maybe several ropes together, in great harmony and with great care for each other, your motions related to what everyone else has to do and can do to the point of ascending. The real mysticism of mountaineering is the body/mind practice of moving on a vertical plane in a realm that is totally inhospitable to human beings.

From many people I learned the practice of how to handle your tools, clean them, put them back; how to work together with other men and women; how to work as hard as you can when it's time for you to work, and how to play together afterwards. I learned this from the people to whom I dedicated my first book, *Riprap*. I came also to a specific spiritual practice, Buddhism, which has some extraordinary teachings within it. The whole world is practicing together; it is not rare or uncommon for people who are living their lives in the world, doing the things they must do, if they have not been degraded or oppressed, to be fully conscious of the dignity and pride of their life and their work. It's largely the fellaheen oppression and alienation that is laid down on people by certain civilized societies throughout history that breaks up people's original mind, original wisdom, the sense and sanity of their work and life. From that standpoint Buddhism, like Christianity, is responding to the alienation of a fragmented society. In doing this, Buddhism developed a *sangha,* which is celibate as a strategy to maintain a certain kind of teaching that in a sense goes against the grain of the contemporary civilization, but will not go *too* much against the grain because it's a survival matter.

135

The larger picture is the possibility that humanity has more original mind from the beginning than we think. Part of our practice is not just sitting down and forming useful little groups within the society but, in a real Mahayana way, expanding our sense of what has happened to us all into a realization that natural societies are in themselves communities of practice. The community of practice that is right at the center of Buddhism, and Hinduism also, is the Neolithic cattle-herding proto-Brahmin family that sang the Vedas together, morning and night. The singing of the Vedas by a group of people, in the family/household, is what lies behind all of the mantras, chants, sutras, and ceremonies that go on all over the Hindu-Buddhist world today. It all goes back to nine thousand years ago, when families sat down and sang together. The yogic practices and meditation come through a line of teaching concerned with life, death, and healing.

To me, the natural unit of practice is the family. The natural unit of the play of practice is the community. A *sangha* should mean the community, just as the real Mahayana includes all living beings. There is cause and consequence. On one level, Theravadin Buddhism says, "Life is suffering, and we must get out of the Wheel"—that's position of cause. But from position of consequence we can say, "The life cycle of creation is endless. We watch the seasons come and go, life into life forever. The child becomes parent, who then becomes our respected elder. Life, so sacred; it is good to be a part of it all." That's an American Indian statement that also happens to be the most illuminated statement from the far end of Buddhism, which does not see an alienated world that we must strive to get out of, but a realized world, in which we know that all plays a part.

Still, so far I've been making my points on practice and original mind from the standpoint of culture and history. That must be done as a corrective, because almost no one understands what civilization is, what it has done, and what the alternatives could be. But I'm not saying an "ideal society" would mean no more work, no more practice, all enlightened play. We still have to get at something called the *kleshas*—obstacles, poisons, mixed-up feelings, mean notions, angriness, sneaky exploitations. Buddhism evolved to deal with these. We're born with them; I guess they come with the large brain super-survival ego sense this primate climaxes with. Maybe all that ego-survival savvy was evolutionary once; now it's counterrevolutionary. But whether we say "Meditate and follow the Buddhadharma" or "Work well and have gratitude to Mother Earth," we're getting at these poisons; that's what the shaman's healing song is all about.

CHOWKA: The place where you've settled—your home in the northern California Sierras—is important to your practice.

SNYDER: Where I live, there is a friendly number of people, diverse as they are, who have a lot of the same spirit. Because we are together in the same part of the world and expect to be together there for the next two or three thousand years, we hope to coevolve our strengths and help each other learn. That cooperation and commitment is in itself practice. In addition, many of the people there have a background in one or another school of Buddhism or Hinduism (although the constellation by which we playfully describe the possibilities is Zen/Hopi/Jew).

Some people in the world don't have to do a hundred thousand prostrations, because they do them day by day in work with their hands and bodies. All over the world there are people who are doing their sitting while they fix the machinery, while they plant the grain, or while they tend the horses. And they *know* it; it's not unconscious. Everybody is equally smart and equally alive.

Where I am, we love occasions to come together. We have a little more time now that we've gotten some of our main water system, fence building, and house building done; we now have the chance to sit together, dance together, and sing together more often.

THE BIOREGIONAL ETHIC

Michael Helm conducted the following interview in early 1979 in Berkeley. It first appeared in the magazine Helm edits, City Miner *(Vol. 4), a bold, struggling little magazine, community-oriented, with its emphasis on the issues, people, and events of the San Francisco Bay Area.*

HELM: Gary, in recent years you, along with people like Wendell Berry, Raymond Dasmann and Peter Berg, have been in the forefront of urging people to rediscover a sense of place. What does that mean in terms of Northern California? What should our priorities be in terms of identifying with and taking care of this place?

SNYDER: Well, first of all a sense of place, of roots, means more than just settling down in some small town and getting a post office box. Today most non-Native Americans (and a lot of Native Americans too—except in Alaska and Canada) constitute a rootless population of people who are moving about from city to city. This is not typical of the way human beings have lived on the planet for fifty thousand and more years.

So to speak of a sense of place is only to speak of what has been common and natural to human living patterns everywhere up until very recently. What are the benefits from beginning to settle in and take responsibility and pay attention to where we are? The benefits are *economic, ecological,* and *spiritual.*

Economic in that in the long range all of us, all over the world, are going to have to learn to live by photosynthesis and

138

with the watersheds once again. Agri-business, petrochemical infusions into what we could call mining-farming, isn't going to sustain us that much longer. And so a sense of place, of plants, soils, climatic cycles, community of beings in one area are all ancient but also necessary components of the information by which we *actually* live. That is to say, of how we actually get our food.

The *ecological* aspect is related to the fact that no matter how much well-meaning environmental legislation might be passed on the state or federal level—and some very interesting and far-reaching legislation has been passed . . .

HELM: Can you give some specific examples?

SNYDER: Well, the Environmental Protection Agency and related legislation. The requirement that an environmental impact report be prepared for virtually every project of any scale at all. The criteria that have been set for environmental impact statements, and the fact that these things go through a review and hearing process in which citizens can challenge the accuracy and adequacy of these statements, means that we all are, theoretically at least, in a position to have a voice in any proposed change in the environment around us. This is important legislation of an order that has not been enacted anywhere else in the world. The existence of this kind of legislation, and of its mandate from the federal down to the county level, is one of the reasons why it can be said quite truly that no political movement in the United States that came out of left field with so little beginning public support has had as much effect on the whole American political and economic system in such a short time as the environmental movement.

HELM: Of course, opponents of environmental legislation are quick to suggest that the environmental movement is an elitist one and not really representative of the majority will.

SNYDER: That's an argument that developers (*laughter*) will certainly make right away. And the Atomic Energy Commission and the Pentagon and all the other investors in the industrial-technological complex who would like to continue their policy of divide and conquer. Just as they did all through the sixties, using FBI and CIA plants and provocateurs inside the peace movement to split apart the blacks, and whites from other whites, as we're finding out under the Freedom of Information Act.

HELM: That's an important act.

SNYDER: You bet. It's very important. But to continue my point, today these same interests would like the Teamsters, who are part of the same general industrial conspiracy, to say that workers aren't interested in the environment. To deflect us from the fundamental recognition of the fact that the environment is where the People actually live, and it's industrial capitalism that is ripping it off, period.

So to continue my answer to your first question, the *ecological* benefits of bioregionalism, of cultivating a sense of place, are that there will then be a *people* to be the People in the place, when it comes down to the line, in terms of implementing and carrying through legislation as mandated. But we shouldn't forget that no legislation is any better than the ultimate will of the people at the grassroots level to have it happen. We have to recognize that there are many people whom we cannot expect to have a regard for the land because they have worked all their lives as part of the industrial machinery.

HELM: Does this include small-scale activities like placer mining and logging?

SNYDER: Well, it goes by individuals. Small-scale placer mining is of no concern. That's not doing any harm. There's an appropriate everything, appropriate mining and appropriate logging. But the closer it gets to local control and local economics the healthier it gets. Because real people have a stronger interest in not ruining the place. Conversely, if your mining is controlled by Saint Joe Minerals, which has operations going in Rhodesia, South Africa, and California all at the same time, you know not only that all the money is going to be taken away from your area, to banks in Switzerland, or whatever, but also that the owners have no concern for the viability of where you live, later on down the line. They don't care if the area becomes a wasteland. So the ecological benefit of rootedness is that people take care of a place because they realize that they're going to live there for a thousand years or more. They know that they aren't going to be forever moving around. We are really now at the end of that American-Anglo mobility process.

HELM: The end of the tourist mentality?

SNYDER: Tourism is another thing. You know Japanese farmers go on pilgrimages in the off season. Travel and tourism are not contradicted by having a place. But having a place means that somebody is there, is an inhabitant that has stock in the situation.

HELM: In terms of heirs?

SNYDER: In terms of heirs, futures, understandings. If you've planted fruit trees that won't bear for a few years you begin thinking in terms of the future. If you have a set of sophisticated knowledges about the right plants and the right planting season for your garden on a certain elevation on a certain slope—and it comes down to that kind of precision—and you're sending that kind of knowledge to the next generation, you're not going to sacrifice it to just any strip-miner that comes down the road. And this is ultimately how we get our food, by these kinds of detailed understandings and teachings with regard to the delicate propagation of plants which are sensitive to the finest variations in climate and soil. Any true farmer, and practically nobody else, understands this. The fact that most of us don't understand this is a measure of our curious and anomalous way of being in the world, of our alienation.

And this leads me to the third benefit, the *spiritual* one, that we get by having a sense of place. Because by being in place, we get the largest sense of community. We learn that community is of spiritual benefit and of health for everyone, that ongoing working relationships and shared concerns, music, poetry, and stories all evolve into the shared practice of a set of values, visions, and quests. That's what the spiritual path really is.

HELM: What do you think is the optimal size for a community?

SNYDER: Well, that would depend on the nature of the region and the economic support base. Northern California is a very diverse landscape with many complex drainages. It's not easy to travel through a lot of it on foot, or even horseback. It tends toward a mosaic of communities rather than a vast spreading of similarities as in a grasslands or desert area. The California landscape slows down the diffusion of stories and skills because each microclimate has its own demands. You have different patterns of oak and conifers, different agricultures. I imagine an interesting, diverse, ultimately agrarian base for Northern California that would not be unlike, say, the classically established agricultural and community patterns of upland Spain, the Pyrenees, or other parts of the Mediterranean, including upland Tunisia, would be one possible model. In terms of community dynamics, I'd say about two hundred people can keep track of each other. More than that and you should probably have two meetings. One for every two hundred people. And occasionally federalize those into "a Thing" as the Icelandic people used to call it.

HELM: What about the Bay Area as a unit? There are over four and a half million people living in the surrounding counties of Alameda, Contra Costa, San Mateo, Marin, and Santa Clara. Are there too many people?

SNYDER: I think it's clearly too many people, that is, if we want a healthy, sustaining environment. A broad spectrum of environmental health would include full presence of fauna, and suitable nonagricultural space for plant community diversity. Populations can and eventually may come down as a matter of choice, of people slowing down their birthrates. It's instructive to remember that the whole area around San Francisco Bay and north into Sonoma and Napa counties was the most densely populated area in North America north of the Rio Grande prior to white arrival.

HELM: How realistic is it that we can actually reduce population? How are you dealing with this in Nevada City, which is one of the fastest-growing areas in the state?

SNYDER: Well, we've had experience with how difficult it is to set guidelines for growth, especially when the paid public officials see no reason, for the most part, why growth shouldn't continue. The fact is that the dynamics of industrial capitalism are still so enormous that until it slows down of its own glut there isn't much we can do except holding actions, and to try to keep our heads clear about what can be and should be. But I have no illusions about the difficulty. I also think it's fairly clear that the existing system stumbles of its own ignorance, particularly on energy and food production. And as it does so we would be well advised to have in mind what kinds of skills we really need and what it means to be self-governing, and to increasingly take responsibility for our own lives, our own neighborhoods, and our own communities.

HELM: Something like the Integral House of the Farrallones Institute as an urban example?

SNYDER: The Integral House is just the very beginning probe into the possibilities of a healthy life here. You know, there's nothing wrong with cities. The only problem with American cities is that they're not really cities.

HELM: What do you mean by that?

SNYDER: I mean that they don't have any of the good qualities of cities, with the exception of some parts of San Francisco, and that they have all the bad qualities of the suburbs. A city should be a convivial place in which you can get everywhere on foot, and where you can come and find your friends, good food, good music, good gambling, good poetry readings without having to own a car or travel great distances from your workplace to the downtown. They should have all of those characteristics of earlier, classical, ancient European cities that are lacking in the American city. A city is obviously a beautiful, functional place. The gardens should go right up to the edge of the city as they used to in Europe. Suburban sprawl is a function of the automobile, the discovery of fossil fuel, and the development of the internal combustion engine. Those things are all beginning to slip into the past even though they are before our eyes yet.

HELM: In a recent interview in *City Miner* Ishmael Reed complained that the environmental movement was elitist and neglected the needs of nonwhite people. He pointed out that the language of environmentalists was technocratic and inaccessible. Why do you think there aren't more blacks, Chicanos, Orientals and Native Americans involved in the environmental movement? How would you respond to Ishmael's criticism that the priority is social justice first and that then nonwhites will get interested in ecology?

SNYDER: I think that what he's saying has some truth in it. Yet the Native American movement, especially if you read back issues of *Akwesasne Notes,* has been profoundly environmental. It has had some of the best articles on the environment that you'll find anywhere. That's because they aspire to be people of *place,* regardless of their poverty. Poverty is not the question. It's rooted or unrooted. Poor people who are in place see what the environmental issues are and respond to them. As the Indian people in Ontario had to respond to the fact of methyl mercury coming into their waters and giving them Minamata disease. (The disease named after the fishing village in Japan in which hundreds of people died and suffered nerve damage from the dumping of methyl mercury into their bay where it subsequently worked its way into their food chain.) The environmental movement in Japan stems from the recognition of local workingmen and fishermen that pollution is killing them. Air pollution in the case of some towns and water pollution, mercury poisoning, as in the town of Minamata. These are working people that cannot get away, go someplace else. They have to take their stand. So, do you see the difference? Ultimately, no matter how empty your stomach is, if you see your child is dying of air pollution-induced asthma, as happens in Japan, then that's important to you, too. So the fact is that it's all one front ultimately. It only serves the interests of the industrial capitalist cancer to have people think it's two fronts, or that environment is white people's concern and jobs poor people's and black people's concern.

Granted, a lot of black people and minority people do have an urban jobless situation that is of course their first priority. But anyone who responsibly goes into these areas as an organizer, as a political activist, who does not also speak of nature and environment as part of the range of their concern, is being

144

politically obtuse, if not downright stupid, in not recognizing the exploitation, the pollution, of the natural world.

The natural world, as anyone should see, is being ripped off, exploited, and oppressed just as our brothers and sisters in the human realm are being exploited and oppressed.

HELM: What about the idea of land reform, a new Homestead Act, as a partial answer to a number of the problems we have been discussing? I recently learned that sixty-one percent of all privately held land in California is owned by some twenty-five corporations. Wouldn't a decentralized, intensive agriculture offer some real possibilities?

SNYDER: Well, we can talk about it and make our plans and our moves but the fact is that agrarian reform will literally take place when the agri-business food production system breaks down. When that system breaks down, then hungry people from the city will be taking, or arranging to give each other, workable farm-size parcels of land out of those huge agri-business holdings. And people will have to do labor-intensive agriculture.

HELM: What kind of time span do you think that's likely to occur in?

SNYDER: I would say anywhere from two decades to a century depending on how the vested interests manage to shuck and jive it. Land reform is inevitable. But the interesting question is do we just stop at a Homestead Act, forty acres and a mule concept—which was originally hasty and ill-advised in its own way—or do people tie that kind of return to actual food production with a community base, a community shared network in which landholding and land sharing devices and forms are more imaginative, such as the land trust concept.

HELM: What are those? Can you go into them in more detail?

SNYDER: The Land Trust concept (and you should know that Huey Johnson, Governor Brown's head of the Department of Resources, is an expert in the field of land trust and was in charge of the Trust for Public Land for some years) means that land is not exactly owned by any individuals but that a trust holds a large parcel of land, or several parcels not necessarily contiguous, managed by a committee, governed by a set of by-

145

laws that define the ways in which the land can be used. Thus the charter will say that this land will be used for orchard, grazing, and vineyard land and x percentage will remain forever forest. The people who live on it will honor this agreement with guaranteed rights as users and as maintainers of the agreement.

HELM: Are there any existing examples of this land trust idea?

SNYDER: Oh yes. It's functioning in California right now, though not in large numbers. It is an idea whose time has certainly come. It's a semicommunitarian landholding device which is legally viable, in which private individuals band together to manage the land somewhat in the way that the federal government manages chunks of land—but on a smaller and more sensitive scale.

HELM: How would you feel about opening up some of the existing public land to private land trust use?

SNYDER: I would much rather see some of the existing farming land, the huge agri-business holdings, do this. The existing public land became "public land" because it was not useful for agriculture. It's essentially tree-growing land. Or in the case of the Bureau of Land Management, it's just brush land a lot of the time. The way the Homestead Act worked, everyone who wanted a homestead grabbed the places that had good soil and water. Theodore Roosevelt and Gifford Pinchot took the rest of the marginal land and made public land out of it, before it could go into the hands of a lot of private developers. That was a good move. So today, there's virtually no land in the national forests that would be viable agriculturally.

HELM: What relationship do you see between living in place and the use of science and technology?

SNYDER: We've always had tools and science. It was science that domesticated the goat, that developed glazed pots, that developed dyes for wool, that domesticated all the vegetables in our gardens and trees in our orchards. That was all accomplished in the Neolithic period, before the dawn of civilization.

146

HELM: That was all soft science though.

SNYDER: I don't know why you say that because "soft" is a word in our culture that has pejorative connotations. What is soft about breeding animals or domesticating trees?

HELM: I was thinking of steel-based technologies.

SNYDER: Well, when you castrate a sheep or a horse I'll tell you it's not a soft operation. What I'm really saying is that technology and science are straw men. The question is, who is being served by them? A small number of owners who have centralized it, production, the banks, and even the government so to speak? Or a technology that is bioregionally appropriate and serves the needs of the people at the same time?

Of course there is a potential technology for the latter. It would have developed considerably longer ago if it had not been to the disadvantage of centralized economies to explore solar technologies. To take a concrete example, small-scale decentralized hydroelectric plants that will run an entire ranch are being produced by an outfit up in the state of Washington. You can stick it in your creek and it will generate all the electricity you need. That could have been made for the last seventy years. PG&E didn't want it. It took a creative company of probably freaks to finally actually put it on the line, to make it marketable so that now you can go and buy it. That's so exciting, the possibilities of energy decentralization. Aldous Huxley wrote that book, *After Many a Summer Dies the Swan,* years ago, in the thirties, in which he said the same thing. A decentralized energy technology could set us free. It's only the prevailing economic and government policies that block us from exploring that further. There is a people's technology. This means that in eight or nine years where we live up in the Sierras without electricity but tied to buying that fifty-five gallon drum of kerosene for our lights, we'll have photovoltaic solar cells charging a couple of car batteries: which will be essentially free energy once the investment of the cells is on the roof. And everybody could do that. We'll do it sooner because we're not wired in.

HELM: Let's talk about larger threats to the environment. What are the major dangers that you see?

SNYDER: The biggest question is, of course, what would come about if nuclear power got going on a large scale. Nuclear power holds the possibility of sustaining a centralized economy a bit longer.

HELM: That's why corporate capitalism wants it.

SNYDER: Of course. But it has scary, unhealthy extensions, namely, radioactive waste disposal for which we have no technology. Also, it has tendencies toward the police state, especially if we go into the breeder reactor, because of the difficulty of policing plutonium. So nuclear energy represents steps in the wrong direction.

HELM: What about nuclear fusion as an alternative?

SNYDER: My informants say forget it. Even if it were technically possible I would still say forget it, because we obviously have not demonstrated our wisdom or capacity to deal with unlimited energy. Unlimited, centralized energy would mean, in my view, unlimited authoritarianism and totalitarianism. It would require a centralized priesthood of guys running it who would constitute a class apart, a set of informations with access to unlimited energy. And Howard T. Odum, a scientist from Florida, says that thermodynamic principles indicate that we would burn ourselves off the earth with an unlimited source of energy, because unlimited energy would generate unlimited waste heat which would in turn raise the temperature of the earth and change the climate.

HELM: What about solar energy from space satellites? Wouldn't the introduction of energy from there do the same thing?

SNYDER: That's a cost-effective question, primarily. Is the net energy gained going to pay for the cost of maintaining that technology in space? Especially if your choice is between decentralized, cottage industry solar energy systems, and centralized, militarized ones controlled by NASA. If it were anywhere near an even choice you would opt for the cottage industry alternative because it would be politically and sociologically healthier.

HELM: What about space colonies, what is your feeling about them?

SNYDER: I think they are unimaginative.

HELM: Unimaginative?

SNYDER: Unimaginative. We've done it already. Why play with that idea anymore. It's a much greater challenge to learn, finally, how to apply our contemporary scientific inclination to refine our biological understandings. To realize that our technologies and all our refinements are crude compared to what plants and photosynthesis are able to do, or compared to what takes place in the process of digestion in any body. We should learn to work with biology rather than to clumsily reconstruct it with nuts and bolts. In a nutshell, our future options are technocratic solutions or sophisticated biological solutions. The second, of course, is obviously right. Biology is preferable to gross technocratic approaches.

HELM: From the point of view of *Gaia* would you also say that it was morally reprehensible to choose the technocratic solution?

SNYDER: Of course. But the fact that it is unimaginative is even worse. Advocates of space colonization say that it is the expression of our great vision, of man's quest, to get on a machine out into space. But the human quest in a spiritual sense is not to be resolved by getting on trains or riding in airplanes. Obviously something that goes into matters of character, commitment, and personal psychology isn't going to be dealt with any better in space than here on earth.

HELM: What are your reflections on having served on the Arts Council in California?

SNYDER: I went onto the Arts Council because I thought it was a really excellent opportunity to stand inside the fence for a while instead of being on the outside throwing rocks as I had always done before. So I wanted to see what it was like to be on the inside and having rocks thrown at you and also see if there was anything that you could do by being in that position, of doing quote "good." The answer is, as you would expect, very complicated. There are some very dedicated, competent people with great skills who labor away in the realms of bureaucracy. And if you make that choice and you are a person with ideals and values you will have to settle for very small achievements, very small gains. Nonetheless, the gains that you make are real gains.

HELM: Can you give a specific example?

SNYDER: Well, creative legislation is an example. You can spend years trying to get a law passed, but when you succeed it's really there. For prophetic-mythic rhetorical poets and radical rhetoricians it ain't nearly enough for ten years of your life's work. On the other hand it's real. Whereas some people have shouted and yelled for ten years and don't have anything to show for it. So that's the other side of it.

In terms of an example, California recently passed a law, initiated by Alan Sieroty, to feed back a little money to painters and other artists for an art object that changed hands at a much higher rate than what it originally sold for. Thus, if you sell a painting for a thousand dollars and it is later sold for fifty thousand dollars, the law now requires that you be paid a royalty on that appreciation. This law is essentially a resale act designed to give greater equity to artists in the commercial process. The art dealers, of course, hate it. Even though, on the face of it, it is a very just law. Eventually, I think this law will be adopted on a federal level. But California led the way.

HELM: What was the Council pushing for while you were on it?

SNYDER: We pushed for bringing working artists and communities together. And let me say that Chairman Peter Coyote deserves a medal and a halo for the enormous amount of work and imagination he has put into this. We wanted to spread the sense that the arts belong to all of us, that we are all participants in the creative process. We wanted to break away from the prevalent idea that only some people are "talented" and they become artists and live in San Francisco working in opera and ballet and the rest of us should be satisfied with watching television. We wanted to encourage the living, creative activities in local high schools and community centers and the diversification of small-scale poetry readings and art shows. We really worked hard toward that end, and I think it is very healthy.

HELM: One of the provisions of public funding has been that you have to have nonprofit status to apply. A lot of people haven't been able to afford the legal fees and time necessary to obtain that status. How do you feel about that?

SNYDER: Well, you have to have some guarantees when you're giving taxpayers' money that it isn't going to someone who is just in business for profit. That's also part of the game. In actual fact, my advice to anyone with energy and creative intent is to bypass the grants process and hustle the money your own way. You'll save yourself a lot of time and heartache. Additionally, it's not much fun to fill out a bunch of forms. I think the private sector has yet to be exploited as well as it can be. Artists should learn how to hustle the way that businessmen do, or at least make things pay for themselves.

HELM: Are there any exceptions to that?

SNYDER: Sure, there are exceptions. For example, opera and ballet cannot pay their own way. They play to full houses; it's not that they don't have an audience, but even at the prices they charge with full houses they operate in the red. That's because they are extremely expensive things to produce. They do not benefit from the fossil fuel subsidy. You can't automate rehearsals for the symphony. There's no way to speed up the production. It's not like modern media events where a lot of it is done by flicking switches. So our society makes a choice as to whether these kinds of labor-intensive art forms are worth supporting. So far, the taxpayers seem to want to keep them going. If you paid the actual value of an opera performance, your ticket would be close to fifty dollars. Now, some people say let's drop those art forms. The fact is that there is still enough of a sense of a cultural history so that people want them to go on, for some time yet. What we try to do is fund in a way that helps these art forms develop a bigger audience, become more self-sustaining. About the time that we go back to intensive farming, the opera will be able to pay its own way once again. You know, the opera was self-supporting in nineteenth-century San Francisco. But that was before the fossil fuel subsidy.

HELM: What's your view about subsidizing literature?

SNYDER: Literature is a funny case. It has a fair chance to make it in the market. It's not too expensive to print a book. If you can't sell three thousand copies, you probably shouldn't have bothered in the first place. If there aren't three thousand people who want your book in the world, then you haven't assessed your audience. If you do sell three thousand copies, you're going to break even, probably make a buck. So I don't see the necessity of grants for literary productions most of the time. The possible exception is if you want to go into very fine, labor-intensive printing—fine paper with fine letterpress printing—then you're getting out of the market. In that case some of the financial support that comes down from the National Endowment is well intended.

HELM: A lot of people will argue that unless you personally sell on the streets, you really can't bring your books to market because of the tie-up and control of distribution by corporate publishing. Many distributors and stores won't carry a book unless you have a whole line of books to offer.

SNYDER: Well, even if you have a grant to print your book, you still are going to have the problem of distributing it. So then you'll wind up with a garage full of unread books. Grants don't really solve that problem. You still have to find out how to distribute and build your own outlets. But there are ways to distribute books; almost every major city has at least two or three outlets for small press books. You just have to do the work and find out who and where they are. Even through these limited outlets, if you pursue them and have something worthwhile, you will sell two to three thousand copies over the course of a few years. So it can be done. Publishing does not need to be a subsidized art in my opinion, even poetry.

HELM: As a result of your appointment to the Arts Council you've had contact with Governor Brown. He seems to be gearing up to run for President. What are your feelings about him as a potential President?

SNYDER: All I know is that I and some other people have been able to have intelligent conversations with Jerry Brown in which our concerns could be voiced and he could speak back to them. I don't know any other politician that I could seriously talk to.

HELM: So that puts him in a league by himself in terms of politicians?

SNYDER: In terms of our actual experience of being able to interact with the man, yes. I don't pretend to understand why he does all the things he does. Anyone of us could invent an ideal President, but in fact, who is interesting? Not ideal, but interesting.

Either you do politics or you don't. A politician is by definition a survivor. If a politician is a man of principle there would be a point where he would be willing to commit political suicide rather than win. Obviously Jerry hasn't reached that point yet. He didn't feel like committing political suicide over Proposition 13. And it *would* have been suicide to continue opposing it. I don't blame him for his position in this particular case. Yet it must be said: skillful political survival is not enough. What makes a politician more than "interesting" is a kind of leadership that takes real risks in the name of what's right. *Leading,* in this case, into a post-high-energy future. And, having the heart to take risks, to lead, is also to show real respect for people—I hope Jerry will take this leap.

HELM: Let's talk about Zen in terms of where it is now and your relation to it.

SNYDER: We all realize by now that Zen is not aesthetics, or haiku, or spontaneity, or minimalism, or accidentalism, or Japanese architecture, or green tea, or sitting on the floor, or samurai movies (*laughter*). It's a way of using your mind and practicing your life and doing it with other people. It has a style that involves others. It brings a particular kind of focus and attention to work. It values work. It values daily life. It values such old-fashioned terms as responsibility and commitment. At the same time it has no external law for doing it. So you must go very deep into yourself to find the foundation of it. In other words it turns you inward rather than giving you a rule book to live by. Zen is a practice that is concerned with *liberation,* not with giving people some easy certainty.

153

HELM: Why did you choose this particluar path as opposed to some form of Christianity in the spiritual sense?

SNYDER: I never knew any Christians. If I had, I might have chosen a path from this tradition. But it wasn't likely, because part of my turning toward the Far East came out of some very intense personal experiences that I had as a young man in direct relation to nature. Face-to-face experience of something else happening from a connection to mountains, forests, and animals. Hair-raising experiences, in some cases. So, I spent a lot of time looking, in this culture and others, to see if anybody knew how to talk about these things.

HELM: Can you give any examples, or would I be intruding?

SNYDER: No, I really can't. Except there are songs that you hear (*laughter*). There is a sense of communication with all of life's network that somehow happens in the wilderness for some people, and I'm one of them. That's where you first learn how to hear: in the wilderness, because the voice and music is clearer there than anywhere else. There's less static there.

Anyhow, those personal moments led me to studying both American Indian and Far Eastern lore. And to ultimately take up the practice of Buddhism as a cosmopolitan and accessible mode of practice. The more I did it, the more I trusted it.

HELM: As you know, people like Leslie Silko and Gerald Hobson (in the *Yardbird Readers*) have been critical of you and other white scholars and poets for what they perceive as an inauthentic ripoff of Native American culture. They accuse you, though more so others, of cultural imperialism in the adoption of the persona of white shaman/healer in your work.

SNYDER: Well, I think Mr. Hobson has a profound misunderstanding when he views a shaman as a cultural artifact. His idea is that a shaman is an Indian thing. There are plenty of Indians who never understood what a shaman was. Or to put it more clearly, they knew what a shaman was but they didn't know where that power came from. There are many primitive peoples for whom the social nexus is the major part of their lives. To step outside of that and make contact with a totally nonhuman other is where a certain kind of power, wisdom, and experience comes from. That is what I'm talking about when I talk about shamanism, which is a worldwide phenomenon and not limited in a proprietary sense to any one culture.

But let me add that a lot of people who use the language of shamanism and write poems that look sort of natural and wild, invoking this and that, have no experience whatsoever of what they write. They have never actually seen the glint in the eye of an eagle or the way a lizard's ribs quake when he does push-ups, or the way a trout turns and flicks, or how a bear backs up. If you haven't seen these things you shouldn't write about them, whether you're an Indian or a white man. And there are a lot of contemporary urban Indians who haven't seen them either.

So to be honest we should confess that most of us are twentieth-century waifs, rootless, and as attached to liberal white values as anyone else. To invoke the term "imperialism" is to invoke the liberal value system of Europe. But in this case the term isn't very interesting anyway because in poetry we all know we are free to lovingly use anything that's available. Nobody is going to say "you shouldn't write in English because your parents were Shoshone." Nobody is going to get on Scott Momaday's case because in his earlier writings he might have written like a Cambridge don or to tell him, "You're an Indian, man, you should write like you wore buckskins." Nobody is going to get on my case because I don't write like a Lutheran just because my great-great-grandparents were maybe Lutherans. That would really be tiresome. As artists we are all free to write about anything we like. And if it is inauthentic it will show up sooner or later. If it really works, then people will trust it.

Shamanism relates to the most archaic of human religious practices. All of our ancestors—white, black, mongoloid, Veddah, or !Kung—were doing it for most of prehistory. It informs the fundamental lore of the planet, that is to say, all of the worldwide body of folktale that we all share. The folk motifs of Native America are scattered all across Europe and Asia. We are all in the same boat, stemming from ten to thirteen thousand years back in the Pleistocene. We are all sharing the same information and the same religious disciplines. It is to the credit of some peoples, like the Native North Americans, that they kept it going longer, and I think they were right. We must all work to help them keep their lands and cultures together. It is to the discredit of other peoples, like our European forebears, that they got led down the garden path of centralized government, civilization, and alienation. But now we have to deal with that and ultimately we may learn something from it.

But the practice of shamanism in itself has at its very center a teaching from the nonhuman, not a teaching from an Indian medicine man, or a Buddhist master. The question of culture does not enter into it. It's a naked experience that some people have out there in the woods.

Coming back to Buddhism, the marvelous perspective of Mahayana—namely the realization that in an oppressive, civilized, cosmopolitan, pluralized first-century A.D. world they might as well be open—has made it capable of being available to everyone while at the same time keeping the strictness and rightness of its own training method. That's a great gift, an institution and tradition that can do that, to be both open and not to have compromised too much historically.

HELM: The body of your work is informed by a tradition. Everything from Chinese Han Shan, *Cold Mountain Poems,* to Zen, to ecology. Do you think that it is necessary for a poet to write out of a tradition?

SNYDER: That tradition is *not* really there unless you make it so. I'm speaking from a lot of sources, from what I've learned. But it's like the air. It's free and there for all of us. Just as Coyote is free for all of us. Coyote doesn't belong to anybody. Coyote is the trickster. The trickster is an archetype inside all of us. There's no cultural monopoly on any of this. What I have done is draw from what I perceive to be certain consistencies that led in the direction of a certain kind of health and sanity, of a certain kind of vision, wherever I found them. And that's been deliberate.

HELM: In the sense of healing?

SNYDER: Well, only in the sense of making whole, which is

the root, the cognate connection, of the word, heal. I'm obviously not a doctor. I'm not doing magic on anybody's head, either. I'm simply striving to get our heads clear to certain wholenesses that are there anyway; like our oneness with nature, the oneness of mind and body, the oneness of conscious and unconscious, our oneness in society with each other. These are basic and ancient conditions from which we flourish.

HELM: Well, what about a writer like Charles Bukowski who dwells on the attraction, perhaps the necessity of, dissipation and escape. You don't find a nature image anywhere in his poetry.

SNYDER: Sure you do. Bukowski is a big animal . . . on the toilet. I love Charles's poems. He manifests a kind of human biology right there. You know, eating, drinking, farting. What could be more natural? (*Laughter.*)

HELM: Is there any subject matter that is taboo to a poet? That one could say was evil?

SNYDER: Oh, of course not. There are things which would be wrong like dishonesties and inauthenticities and posturing. But that's just bad poetry. There might also be bad politics. But that has to be dealt with in another way.

HELM: What about the printed word in terms of the future? Do you think that as we begin living in more natural ways that it will fade into disuse?

SNYDER: I can't imagine that it would. The printed word is such a convenient and low tech way of storing language that once we have it it will hang around forever. But that doesn't mean that it's always a good thing. I was reading a paper by an ethnolinguist couple, Ron and Suzie Scollon, who are working with native people up in Alaska and Canada, and they have a paper on literacy as a "state of mind" that is fascinating. It shows the profound differences in the way that literate and nonliterate people use language, live in the world, and see the world. The nonliterate way of seeing is truly centered and focused. But conversely, the literate way of seeing has all the capacity for accepting plurality, for dealing with diverse human situations, and that's why it survives. Isolated, focused enclaves, however beautiful they may be, have tremendous problems when they run into the pluralistic world of trade, guns, alcohol, wire, transistor radios, snowmobiles, Cokes. The first thing they run into is many possible values—"there is another way to do it."

HELM: In terms of Northern California, do you think it would be desirable for it to become politically autonomous?

SNYDER: Certainly more autonomous. That old federalist idea maybe wasn't a bad one. Ultimately, what I would like to see is all of the political boundaries of Turtle Island rethought to more appropriate bioregional lines. We would have Northern California, Central California and Southern California. Or maybe Northern California and Southern Oregon as one; Northern Oregon and Southern Washington as one; Northern Washington and Southern British Columbia. They all constitute natural foci. We could go through the whole landscape and redo it right. I think that it will be done, someday, maybe a thousand years from now.

HELM: As someone who was born in San Francisco, it seems appropriate to end with your thoughts about this place. What would you like to say about it, or to us?

SNYDER: San Francisco taught me what a city could be, and saved me having to go to Europe!

POETRY, COMMUNITY & CLIMAX

The following text is based on talks given at Oberlin College and Brown University in the fall of 1978. It was first published in Field 20 (*Spring, 1979*).

I

I wrote a small piece ten years ago called "Poetry and the Primitive." It was subtitled "Notes on Poetry as an Ecological Survival Technique." In a brisk and simple way, I was trying to indicate what modern people might want to learn and use from the way poetry/song works in a strong, self-contained preliterate society. I have also spoken of poetry's function as an occasional voice for the nonhuman rising within the human realm, and the value of that. Survival.

But it's clear now, 1979, that survival is not exactly the problem. Not for human beings, who will survive come hell or high water—and both may—to find themselves sole operators of the equipment on a planet where vertebrate evolution has come to an end. Clouds of waterfowl, herds of bison, great whales in the ocean, will be—almost are—myths from the dreamtime, as is, already, "the primitive" in any virgin sense of the term. Biological diversity, and the integrity of organic evolution on this planet, is where I take my stand: not a large pretentious stand, but a straightforward feet-on-the-ground stand, like my grandmother nursing her snapdragons and trying at grafting apples. It's also inevitably the stand of the poet, child of the Muse, singer of saneness, and weaver of rich fabric to delight the mind with possibilities opening both inward and outward.

There is a huge investment in this nation: bridges, railway tracks, freeways, downtown office buildings, airports, aircraft carriers, miles of subdivisions, docks, ore-carriers, factories. All that belongs to somebody, and they don't want to see it become useless, unprofitable, obsolete. In strict terms of cash flow and energy flow it still works, but the hidden costs are enormous and those who pay that cost are not the owners. I'm speaking of course not only of human alienation but air and water, stands of trees, and all the larger, more specialized, rarer birds and animals of the world who pay the cost of "America" with their bodies—as mentioned above. To keep this investment working, the several thousand individuals who own it have about convinced the rest of us that we are equal owners with them of it; using language like "don't turn out the lights," "let's not go back to the Stone Age," and "you've worked hard for what you got, don't lose it now." Their investment requires continual growth, or it falters. A "steady state economy" and "small is beautiful" are terrifying concepts for them because without growth, the gross inequalities in the distribution of wealth in this land would become starkly clear. From this it's evident that the future of capitalism and perhaps all industrial society is intimately staked on the question of nuclear energy—no other way to keep up growth. This leads to the disastrous fast breeder reactor (which is not dead yet by a long shot), and the fast breeder leads to a police state. But food shortages may bring it down even before energy shortages—the loss of soils and the growing inefficiencies of chemical fertilizers.

I repeat this well-known information to remind us, then, that monoculture—heavy industry, television, automobile culture—is not an ongoing accident; it is deliberately fostered. Any remnant city neighborhood of good cheer and old friendships, or farming community that "wants to stay the way it is" are threats to the investment. Without knowing it, little old ladies in tennis shoes who work to save whooping cranes are enemies of the state, along with other more flamboyant figures. I guess there are revolutionaries who still hope for their own kind of mono-cultural industrial utopia, however. And there are some for whom alienation is a way of life, an end in itself. It's helpful to remember that what we'd hope for on the planet is creativity and sanity, conviviality, the real work of our hands and minds: those apples and snapdragons. Existential *angst* won't go away nohow, if that's how you get your energy.

Although it's clear that we cannot again have seamless primitive cultures, or the purity of the archaic, we can have neighborhood and community. Communities strong in their sense of place, proud and aware of local and special qualities, creating to some extent their own cultural forms, not humble or subservient in the face of some "high cultural" over-funded art form or set of values, are in fact what one healthy side of the original American vision was about. They are also, now, critical to "ecological survival." No amount of well-meaning environmental legislation will halt the biological holocaust without people who live where they are and work with their neighbors, taking responsibility for their place, and *seeing to it:* to be inhabitants, and to not retreat. We feel this to be starting in America: a mosaic of city neighborhoods, small towns, and rural places where people are digging in and saying "if not now, when? if not here, where?" This trend includes many sorts of persons, some of whom are simply looking out for themselves and finding a better place to live. The process becomes educational, and even revolutionary, when one becomes aware of the responsibility that goes with "rootedness" and the way the cards are stacked against it; we live in a system that rewards those who leap for the quick profit and penalizes those who would do things carefully with an eye to quality. Decentralization could start with food production. Old/new-style biologically sophisticated farming doesn't imply total local self-sufficiency, but at least the capacity to provide food and fiber needs within a framework of two or three hundred miles. Then come new definitions of territory and region, and fresh ways to see local government limits—watershed politics, bioregion consciousness. Sense of community begins to include woodpeckers and cottontails. Decentralization includes the decentralization of "culture," of poetry.

II

Now to speak of twenty-five years of poetry readings in the U.S. When I was working on the docks in San Francisco and occasionally taking night courses in conversational Japanese around '52 or '53, writing poems and sending them off to magazines, *Kenyon Review,* and *Hudson Review* and *Partisan,* and getting them back, we had no sense of a community of poets and even less of an audience. Kenneth Rexroth held open house in his apartment on Friday evenings, and four or five or sometimes ten people might drop by; some out of an old Italian anarchist group, some from the filmmakers' and artists' circles of the Bay Area. In 1954 I knew virtually every poet, filmmaker, and artist in the region. I hardly know who works in Berkeley anymore, let alone the rest.

In 1955, because Allen Ginsberg and Philip Whalen, Michael McClure, Philip Lamantia and several others, and myself, found ourselves with large numbers of unpublished poems on our hands, it occurred to us to give a poetry reading. It was like holding a sale. In those days all we ever thought of doing with poetry was to get it published; we didn't know who saw it, and didn't think to offer it up publicly. But we went ahead and organized a poetry reading. We did have a model or two; Dylan Thomas had passed through a year before; Ted Roethke had come down from Seattle and read; the San Francisco Poetry Center had organized a few readings in five or six years. Still, poetry readings were definitely not a part of the cultural and social landscape. That reading held in November, 1955, in a space borrowed from an art gallery, was a curious kind of turning point in American poetry. It succeeded beyond our wildest thoughts. In fact, we weren't even thinking of success; we were just trying to invite some friends and potential friends, and we borrowed a mailing list from the art gallery and sent out maybe two hundred postcards. Poetry suddenly seemed useful in 1955

San Francisco. From that day to this, there has never been a week without a reading in the Bay Area—actually more like three a night, counting all the coffee shops, plus schools, the art museum, the aquarium, and the zoo. Those early readings led to publication for some. *Howl* became the second book in Ferlinghetti's Pocket Poets series, and Ginsberg's extensive early readings all over the United States began to draw audiences of a size not seen before. Kerouac's novels were published, and the "beat generation" was launched. Allen was to a great extent responsible for generating the excitement, but a number of other poets (myself not among them because I had gone to Japan) traveled widely over the United States landing like crows first in coffee houses and later becoming gradually accepted more and more into the network of universities.

One thing that was clearly an error in the mentality of the early fifties literary world was the idea that poetry cannot have an audience, and indeed that it was a little shameful if a poem was too popular. There are people who still believe that, incidentally. There was also the defeatist attitude that "we live in a philistine culture" and "no one is interested in art anyway, so we'll just write to each other." My generation found that boldly, to put it bluntly, having something to say helped with audiences. It also should be apparent that one is not *owed* an audience by the culture; but one can indeed go out and try to build an audience. Building that audience is done in part by going on the road and using your voice and your body to put the poems out there; and to speak to the people's condition, as the Quakers would say, to speak to the conditions of your own times, and not worry about posterity. If you speak to the condition of your times with some accuracy and intention, then it may speak to the future, too. If it doesn't, fine, we live in the present. So poetry readings as a new cultural form enhanced and strengthened poetry itself, and the role of the poet. They also taught us that poetry really is an oral art. It would be fascinating to undertake an examination of how poetry of the last twenty years has been shaped by the feedback that comes with reading in front of people. Poems go through revisions, adaptations and enhancements following on the sense of how audiences have been hearing you. So there is a communal aspect to the evolution of the art. Does this mean that poets, knowing that they were writing for an audience, might have catered to that possibility? Sure. But it also means that audiences have come up to the possibility of hearing better over the years. My experience is that the latter tends to be the case and that audiences have grown in maturity and the poetry with them. With a skilled audience, such as you often find in New York or San Francisco (and recently in Midwestern cities like Minneapolis), the poet knows that he/she can try for more, and really push it to the difficult, the complex, the outrageous, and see where the mind of the people will go.

This practice of poetry reading has had an effect on the poets who were quite content to regard poetry as a written art that sits on a printed page and belongs in libraries, too. They have been forced to actually learn how to read poetry aloud better out of sheer competition if nothing else. There are economic rewards involved.

Poetry belongs to everybody, but there are always a few skilled raconteurs or creators or singers, and we live in a time in which the individual actor or creator is particularly valued. The art wouldn't die out if we lost track of the name of the fellow who made it up, though, and the fact that we don't know the names of the men or women who made the songs in the past doesn't really matter.

All of this goes one more step, then, to a conscious concern and interest on the part of some poets in the actual performance skills of preliterate people. My own studies in anthropology, linguistics, and oral literature brought me to the realization that the performance, in a group context, is the pinnacle of poetic activity and precision, and we have yet to develop the possibilities of that circle with music, dance, and drama in their original archaic poetic relationship. The Ainu singers of Hokkaido chant their long epic stories to a beat. The güslars of southern Yugoslavia use a little dulcimer-like stringed instrument. No wonder we say "lyric poetry"—they used to sing with a lyre. Most of the songs that you hear on the country and western hit parade are in good old English ballad meter, showing that the ballad is the backbone of English-language poetics and will be for a long time to come. Other examples, simple examples: Robert Bly knows almost all his poems by heart and Roethke knew his. Reciting from memory (which I can't do) liberates your hands and mind for the performance—liberates your eyes. Noh drama, with its aristocratic spareness and simplicity, could be another model. Percussive, almost nonmelodic music is very strong; a bare stage is all you need.

In this era of light shows, huge movie screens, and quadraphonic sound systems, it is striking that an audience will still come to hear a plain, ordinary, unaugmented human being using nothing but voice and language. That tells us that people do appreciate the compression, the elegance, and the myriad imageries that come out of this art of distilling language and giving it measure which is called poetry.

III

The next step then is to ask what has a more public poetry done for the possibility of community? The modern poetry audience has a certain kind of network associated with it. Everywhere I go I meet people I know—from one corner of the United States to the other I never give a reading anymore but at least one person comes out of the audience, an old friend. A dozen other people that I haven't met before step up to tell me about how they are riding their horses or growing sunflowers somewhere, or are in the middle of making a zendo inside an old building downtown. It's a fine exchange of news and information, and also the reaffirmation of a certain set of interests to which I (among others) speak. The community that is called together by such events is not just literary. It's interesting to see, then, that the universities have served as community halls, public space, that draw out people from beyond the immediate academic world. In other times and places such public spaces have been riverbeds—which is no-man's land—where the gypsies and the traveling drama companies are allowed to put up their tents, or where the homeless samurai are allowed to act out their final duels with each other and nobody cares—it might be riverbeds, it might be the streets, or temples and churches—or in the tantric tradition of late medieval north India, some groups met in cemeteries.

What is this network of interests and old friends I speak of? None other than that branch of the stalwart counterculture that has consistently found value and inspiration in poetry, and intellectual excitement in watching the unfolding of twentieth-century poetics. Also certain sets of values have been—in recent decades—more clearly stated in poetry than any other medium. (Other post-World War II cultural branches are primarily affiliated to music; some to more specific and intellectually formulated political or religious ideologies; a few go directly to crafts, or to gardening.) Anyway: the people who found each other via poetry readings in the late fifties and sixties produced another generation of poets who were committed to an oral poetics and a nonelite vision of communicating to larger and more diverse audiences. There are roughly three shoots from that root. I'll call them the dealers, the home-growers, and the ethnobotanists.

The "dealers" came in part with the growth of a certain academic and social acceptance of new poets and their readings, which led to the poetry policies of the NEA; the founding of the little magazines and small presses support organizations, the poets-in-the-schools programs, and on the academic side, several MFA-in-writing programs at several universities; workshops in poetry. At this point, via the poets-in-the-schools programs in particular, twentieth-century poetry began to find its way into ordinary American communities. The programs employed people who had gotten their MFA or a little book published (through a small press, with federal aid often)—and put them into high schools or grade schools, doing creative work, creative word playfulness, image playfulness; generating imagination and spontaneity among school children whose usual

166

teachers couldn't. I consider this quite valid as a mode of poetic imagination and practice, in its broadest sense, filtering down through the population. The school districts themselves, after some resistance, began to accept the possibilities of poets and other artists doing local residencies. For every horror story of a brought-in poet reading a poem to the sixth grade with the word "penis" in it, there are countless unadvertised little openings of voice and eye as children got that quick view of playfulness, of the flexibility and power of their own mind and mother tongue. I've watched this at work in my own school district, which is rural and short on money, but has backed the artists in schools as far as it could. In fact this school district (and many others) has chosen to keep arts programs going even after state or federal funding is withdrawn. One local poet found that what the children needed first was an introduction to the basic sense of story and of lore. He became the master of lore, myth, and word-hoard for the whole district. By much research and imagination, he provided, following the calendar and seasons, the true information—as story—about what Easter, May Day, Christmas, Hanukkah, Halloween, and Lammas are about. Neither the parents nor the school teachers in most cases could provide this fundamental lore of their own culture to the children. The poet was Steve Sanfield, doing the work of mythographer to the community in the ancient way.

The "home-growers" (and the above folks often overlap with this) are those poets who themselves live in a place with some intention of staying there—and begin to find their poetry playing a useful role in the daily life of the neighborhood. Poetry as a tool, a net or trap to catch and present; a sharp edge; a medicine, or the little awl that unties knots. Who are these poets? I haven't heard of most of them, neither have you; perhaps we never will. The mandarins of empire-culture arts organizations in the U.S. might worry about little-known poets working in the schools, because they are afraid of a decline in "standards of quality." I think I am second to none in my devotion to Quality; I throw myself at the lotus feet of Quality and shiver at the least tremor of her crescent moon eyebrow. What they really fear is losing control over the setting of standards. But there is room for many singers, and not everyone need aspire to national level publication, national reputation. The United States is, bioregionally speaking, too large to ever be a comprehensible social entity except as maintained at great expense and effort via the media and bureaucracy. The price people pay for living in the production called American society is that they are condemned to continually watch television and read newspapers to know "what's happening," and thus they have no time to play with their own children or get to know the neighbors or birds or plants or seasons. What a dreadful cost! This explains why I do not even try to keep up with what's going on in nationwide poetry publishing. We are talking about real culture now, the culture that things *grow* in, and not the laboratory strains of seeds that lead to national reputation. Poetry is written and read for real people: it should be part of the gatherings where we make decisions about what to do about uncontrolled growth, or local power plants, and who's going to be observer at the next county supervisors' meeting. A little bit of music is played by the guitarists and five-string banjo players, and some poems come down from five or six people who are really good—speaking to what is happening *here*. They shine a little ray of myth on things; memory turning to legend.

It's also useful to raise a sum of money for a local need with a benefit poetry reading, and it's good to know this can be done successfully maybe twice a year. It works, a paying audience comes, because it's known that it will be a strong event. Sooner or later, if a poet keeps on living in one place, he is going to have to admit to everyone in town and on the backroads that he writes poetry. To then appear locally is to put your own work to the real test—the lady who delivers the mail might be there, and the head sawyer of the local mill. What a delight to mix all levels of poems together, and to see the pleasure in the eyes of the audience when a local tree, a local river or mountain, comes swirling forth as part of proto-epic or myth. (Michael

McClure once said his two favorite provincial literary periodicals were *Kuksu,* "Journal of Backcountry Writing," and *The New York Review of Books.* Two poetry reading invitations that I count as great honors were to the Library of Congress, and the North San Juan Fire Hall.) It is a commitment to place, and to your neighbors, that—with no loss of quality—accomplishes the decentralization of poetry. The decentralization of "culture" is as important to our long-range ecological and social health as the decentralization of agriculture, production, energy, and government.

By the "ethnobotanist" shoot from that sixties root I mean the roving specialists and thinkers in poetics, politics, anthropology, and biology who are pursuing the study of what it would mean to be citizens of natural nations; to be part of stable communities; participants in a sane society. We do this with the point in mind that the goal of structural political change is not a crazy society, but a sane one. These are in a sense studies in postrevolutionary possibilities, and in the possibilities of making small gains now; "forming the new society within the shell of the old." Such are (and though I list them here it doesn't mean they necessarily agree with all or anything I say) Bob Callahan and associates at Turtle Island Foundation; Peter Berg and the Planet Drum group; Joe Meeker, Vine Deloria, Jr., and others working on the "new natural philosophy"; the Farallones Institute; Jerome Rothenberg and the *New Wilderness Newsletter;* Dennis Tedlock and *Alcheringa* magazine; Stewart Brand's *Coevolution Quarterly;* the long list of useful publications from Richard Grossinger and Lindy Hough; the Lindisfarne Association; New Alchemy; and in another more technical dimension, Stanley Diamond's work and his journal *Dialectical Anthropology. Organic Gardening* and other Rodale Press publications, with their consistent emphasis on *health* as the basic measure, might also belong on this list. There are others; I'm not even mentioning poetry magazines in this context. As a sort of ethnobotanist myself, I make the following offering:

169

IV

Poetry as song is there from birth to death.[10] There are songs to ease birth, good luck songs to untie knots to get babies born better; there are lullabies that you sing to put the babies to sleep—Lilith Abye—("get away negative mother image!"); there are songs that children sing on the playground that are beginning poetries—

> baby baby suck your toe
> all the way to Mexico
>
> kindergarten baby
> wash your face in gravy

(I get these from my kids) or

> Going down the highway, 1954,
> Batman let a big one, blew me out the door—
> wheels wouldn't take it,
> engine fell apart,
> all because of Batman's supersonic fart.

(If you start poetry teaching on the grade school level, use rhyme, they love it. Go with the flow, don't go against it. Children love word play, music of language; it really sobered me up to realize that not only is rhyme going to be with us but it's a good thing.) And as we get older, about eleven or twelve years, we go into the work force and start picking strawberries or drying apples; and work songs come out of that. Individually consciously created poetry begins when you start making up love songs to a sweetie, which are called courting songs. Then, some individuals are sent out in adolescence to see if they can get a power vision song all by themselves. They go out and come back with a song which is their own, which gives them a name, and power; some begin to feel like a "singer." There are those who use songs for hunting, and those who use a song for keeping themselves awake at night when they are riding around slow in circles taking care of the cows; people who use songs when they haul up the nets on the beach. And when we get together we have drinking songs and all kinds of communal pleasure gathering group music. There are war songs, and particular specialized powerful healing songs that are brought back by those individuals (shamans) who make a special point of going back into solitude for more songs: which will enable them to heal. There are also some who master and transmit the complex of songs and chants that contain creation-myth lore and whatever ancient or cosmic gossip that a whole People sees itself through. In the Occident we have such a line, starting with Homer and going through Virgil, Dante, Milton, Blake, Goethe, and Joyce. They were workers who took on the ambitious chore of trying to absorb all the myth/history lore of their times, and of their own past traditions, and put it into order as a new piece of writing and let it be a map or model of world and mind for everyone to steer by.

It's also clear that in all the households of nonliterate ordinary farming and working people for the past fifty thousand years the context of poetry and literature has been around the fire at night—with the children and grandparents curled up together and somebody singing or telling. Poetry is thus an intimate part of the power and health of sane people. What then? What of the danger of becoming provincial, encapsulated, self-righteous, divisive—all those things that we can recognize as being sources of mischief and difficulty in the past?

That specialized variety of poetry which is the most sophisticated, and is the type which most modern poetry would aspire to be, is the "healing songs" type. This is the kind of healing that makes whole, heals by making whole, that kind of doctoring. The poet as healer is asserting several layers of larger realms of wholeness. The first larger realm is identity with the natural world, demonstrating that the social system, a little human enclave, does not stand by itself apart from the plants and the animals and winds and rains and rivers that surround it. Here the poet is a voice for the nonhuman, for the natural world, actually a vehicle for another voice, to send it into the human world, saying there is a larger sphere out there; that the humans are indeed children of, sons and daughters of, and eternally in relationship with, the earth. Human beings buffer themselves against seeing the natural world directly. Language, custom, ego, and personal advantage strategies all work against clear seeing. So the first wholeness is wholeness with nature.

The poet as myth-handler-healer is also speaking as a voice for another place, the deep unconscious, and working toward integration of interior unknown realms of mind with present moment immediate self-interest consciousness. The outer world of nature and the inner world of the unconscious are brought to a single focus occasionally by the work of the dramatist-ritualist artist-poet. That's another layer. Great tales and myths can give one tiny isolated society the breadth of mind and heart to be *not* provincial and to know itself as a piece of the cosmos.

The next layer, when it works, is harder: that's the layer that asserts a level of humanity with other people outside your own group. It's harder actually because we are in clear economic dependence and interrelationship with our immediate environment; if you are gathering milkweed, fishing, picking berries, raising apples, and tending a garden it shouldn't be too difficult to realize that you have some relationship with nature. It's less obvious what to do with the folks that live on the other side of the mountain range, speaking another language; they're beyond the pass, and you can faintly feel them as potential competitors. We must go beyond just feeling at one with nature, and feel at one with each other, with ourselves. That's where all natures intersect. Too much to ask for? Only specialists, mystics, either through training or good luck, arrive at that. Yet it's the good luck of poetry that it sometimes presents us with the accomplished fact of a moment of true nature, of total thusness:

> Peach blossoms are by nature pink
> Pear blossoms are by nature white.

This level of healing is a kind of poetic work that is forever "just begun." When we bring together our awareness of the worldwide network of folktale and myth imagery that has been the "classical tradition"—the lore-bearer—of everyone for ten thousand and more years, and the new (but always there) knowledge of the worldwide interdependence of natural systems, we have the biopoetic beginning of a new level of world poetry and myth. That's the beginning for this age, the age of knowing the planet as one ecosystem, our own little watershed, a community of people and beings, a place to sing and meditate, a place to pick berries, a place to be picked in.

The communities of creatures in forests, ponds, oceans, or grasslands seem to tend toward a condition called climax, "virgin forest"—many species, old bones, lots of rotten leaves, complex energy pathways, woodpeckers living in snags, and conies harvesting tiny piles of grass. This condition has considerable stability and holds much energy in its web—energy that in simpler systems (a field of weeds just after a bulldozer) is lost back into the sky or down the drain. All of evolution may have been as much shaped by this pull toward climax as it has by simple competition between individuals or species. If human beings have any place in this scheme it might well have to do with their most striking characteristic—a large brain, and language. And a consciousness of a peculiarly self-conscious order. Our human awareness and eager poking, probing, and studying is our beginning contribution to planet-system energy-conserving; another level of climax!

In a climax situation a high percentage of the energy is derived not from grazing off the annual production of biomass, but from recycling dead biomass, the duff on the forest floor, the trees that have fallen, the bodies of dead animals. Recycled. Detritus cycle energy is liberated by fungi and lots of insects. I would then suggest: as climax forest is to biome, and fungus is to the recycling of energy, so "enlightened mind" is to daily ego mind, and art to the recycling of neglected inner potential. When we deepen or enrich ourselves, looking within, understanding ourselves, we come closer to being like a climax system. Turning away from grazing on the "immediate biomass" of perception, sensation, and thrill; and re-viewing memory, internalized perception, blocks of inner energies, dreams, the leaffall of day-to-day consciousness, liberates the energy of our own sense-detritus. Art is an assimilator of unfelt experience, perception, sensation, and memory for the whole society. When all that compost of feeling and thinking comes back to us then, it comes not as a flower, but—to complete the metaphor—as a mushroom: the fruiting body of the buried threads of mycelia that run widely through the soil, and are intricately married to the root hairs of all the trees. "Fruiting"—at that point—is the completion of the work of the poet, and the point where the artist or mystic reenters the cycle: gives what she or he has done as nourishment, and as spore or seed spreads the "thought of enlightenment," reaching into personal depths for nutrients hidden there, back to the community. The community and its poetry are not two.

SOME FURTHER ANGLES

*The excerpts that follow are from interviews and talks not in-
cluded in their entirety in this collection; two short passages cited
are taken from letters. The numbers refer back to superscript numbers of related passages within the text.*

*Three longer interviews were not collected in this volume because
they are readily available in other publications: an interview with
Ekbert Faas, in his* Towards a New American Poetics *(Santa Barbara: Black Sparrow Press, 1978), pp. 105–142; an interview en-
titled "Moving the World a Millionth of an Inch," in* The Beat
Diary, The Unspeakable Visions of the Individual, *5 (1977), 140–
157; and* On Bread and Poetry, *a panel discussion with Gary
Snyder, Lew Welch and Philip Whalen, ed. Donald Allen (Bolinas:
Grey Fox Press, 1977).*

*For some detail of Snyder's early anthropology studies the reader
is referred to Nathaniel Tarn's "From Anthropologist to Informant:
A Field Record of Gary Snyder," in* Alcheringa, *Old Series, No. 4
(1972), pp. 104–113.*

1 (p. 5) On Snyder's understanding of shamanism see his
comment to Chuck Simmons, in "A Short Talk with Gary Snyder," *Mountain Gazette,* No. 36 (1976), p. 27: "I guess I
would define shamanism as man's basic mind-science and practice from the Upper-Paleolithic down to the beginning of civilization—interesting in that it was empirical, experiential, prag-
matic, and international. Poetry within the civilized area of
history is the fragmented attempt to recreate a 'healing song'
aspect of the shaman's practice."

What Snyder understands by "healing songs" he stated in a talk at Lindisfarne in New York City in April of 1977: "Healing on many levels but not really psychotherapy—healing primarily on the level of continually bringing back in the dreamlore, myth-lore, free-floating/international themes and motifs as concentrated in their place, bringing it back into the consciousness of everybody, to show everyone who they are, and to give people a place."

2 (p. 15) On Snyder's view of the relationship of Hindu and Buddhist thought to archaic religious practice see his comments in Dom Aelred Graham's *Conversations: Christian and Buddhist* (N.Y.: Harcourt, 1968), pp. 74–76: "Vajrayana, of all the sophisticated and learned religious traditions in the world today, seems to be the only one that has traditional continuous links that go back to the Stone Age. Actually Shaivism has that, too. Buddhism itself cuts off the earlier dispensation, but Tantrism brings it back in again. These are the religious insights and practices that belonged to the paleolithic hunters at the beginning. This is the *real* nature mysticism. People who talk about nature mysticism don't know what they're talking about. There have been lots more people in the last two thousand years who have been mystics within the terms of "supernatural" mysticism than there have been people who have known what that real nature mysticism is, who have known really what it is to wear the animal masks and to dance the animal steps. And this has been put down—to be realistic, it's what's been called "witchcraft." And Shiva is, if you get back to his historical roots, probably Satan with his horns and his animal worshipers. He belongs to the mythological stratum that the archetype of Satan comes out of. There are all kinds of curious questions that you get into when you start asserting that the powers of the earth and the powers of the underground are valid powers and that your inspiration belongs to them.

* * *

"The Buddha Dharma strives to escape from the cycle of birth and death, and so does much of the Hindu Dharma. The school of Kali and the Shaktites and some of the Tantric schools accept birth and death in all of their hair-raising possibilities. The poet is right there on that balance, right in there in the area that says "Let the shit fly," which is different from the religious person in civilized times, who is operating in the realm of control, self-discipline, purity, training, self-knowledge."

3 (p. 31) Snyder's present view of Olson's work is well summarized in the following statement, made in a talk on literary genre at San Diego State University (1973): "Charles Olson's poetry is perhaps the best example of a scholarly, intellectual, and wide-ranging poetry. It is, in some sense, a new form of speculative-thinking prose, in which a high density content is being transmitted, powerful stuff, if you understand it that way. It's also very demanding, in the sense that it is not written for anybody to pick up on. It is written for those who want to go far fast and are willing to put out the effort. But for those people who are willing to do that, the rewards are infinitely greater."

4 (p. 37) Urban poetry, as Dan McLeod recalls Snyder saying in conversation, represents for him " 'the poetry of the closeness of people,' always a good subject, and not to be confused with a 'poetry of boredom, disaffection and despair.' " In this conversation (portions of which are reprinted in McLeod's remembrance "Gary Snyder in Hokkaido," *Poetry Nippon,* 21 [1972], 18–21), Snyder "referred to a distinction the poet Denise Levertov once drew between 'intuitive' and 'rational' imagination—the first appropriate for dealing with nature, the second for society."

5 (p. 39) Snyder amplifies a bit on his method of translation in the following letter to Dell Hymes, quoted by Hymes in his article "Some North Pacific Coast Poems: a Problem in Anthropological Philology," *American Anthropologist,* 67 (1965),

335–336: ". . . the problem, in a sense, is not one of 'writing' but one of 'visualizing.' I have found this to be very true of Chinese poetry translation. I get the verbal meaning into mind as clearly as I can, but then make an enormous effort of visualization, to 'see' what the poem says, nonlinguistically, like a movie in my mind, and to feel it. If I can do this (and much of the time the poem eludes this effort) then I write the scene down in English. It is not a translation of the words, it is the same poem in a different language, allowing for the peculiar distortions of my own vision—but keeping it straight as possible. If I can do this to a poem the translation is uniformly successful, and is generally well received by scholars and critics. If I can't do this, I can still translate the words, and it may be well received, but it doesn't feel like it should."

6 (p. 98) On Oda Sesso Roshi (1901–1966) and Snyder's years in Japan see, too, his recollections in *Wind Bell,* 8 (1969), 27: "When Oda Roshi, the Dharma heir of Goto Roshi, became Kancho and also Roshi of the monastery of Daitoku-ji, Goto Roshi said to him, 'You should be open to foreigners,' and so Daitoku-ji became the orthodox Rinzai temple that was open to foreigners as none of the others ever were really and aren't today. Foreigners could come and sit in the monastery and then if they were still around after a year and had learned Japanese, they might be accepted as disciples of Oda Roshi.

"My teacher was Oda Roshi, and I studied with him up until he died in September, 1966. He was originally from a poor farming family in Tottori Prefecture, given to a Zen temple at the age of ten. He was in the Myoshin-ji Sodo for a while and later in Korea with Goto Roshi. I was his first foreign student, I think, and then a young Dutchman named Janwillem van de Wetering was there for almost a year; a man from Jerusalem named Zef ben Shahar and a Guatemalan named Ernesto Falla were his disciples for a while; Irmgard Schloegl was there from 1960 on; and there were a few other people who came and went."

7 (p. 106) In his conversation with Dom Aelred Graham, cited in Note 2 (above), Snyder discussed in some detail the differences between Zen and Tibetan practice (pp. 64–65): "Vajrayana leads a person to enlightenment through the exploitation and development of powers. . . . This is, in Buddhist terms, the Sambhoga-kaya path, the path of the realm of ideal forms and the Bliss body of the Buddha. Zen has proceeded on the Dharma-kaya path, which is the path of emptiness, the path of formlessness. Consequently, in its practice, in working with a Roshi, if you have hallucinations, visions, extraordinary experiences, telepathy, levitation, whatever, and you go to your Roshi, he says, "Pay no attention to it; stick to your koan." So Zen does not explore those realms. Although in the process of Zen studies, koan study, especially in your first koan, when you're doing zazen for many hours, for many weeks or months, you become aware of these different realms, you block yourself from going into them at all. You leave those all behind; they're classified as *mozo,* delusions, in the Zen school. Whereas in Shaivite Yoga and in certain schools of Tibetan Buddhism you take each of those realms up one at a time and explore it as part of your knowledge of yourself. Both of these schools of Buddhism, Zen and Tibetan Buddhism, have the same historical roots, the Madhyamika and the Yogacara. They're both schools of practice. In distinction to the Paramitayanas, both schools assert that it's possible to become enlightened in one lifetime, and that you do not need to perfect yourself in countless lifetimes. So they're extremely close. They're closer than any other schools in Buddhism. However, one proceeds in Zen by going directly to the ground of consciousness, to the contentless empty mirror of the mind, and then afterward, after ten or fifteen years of koan study, coming up bit by bit, using each of the koans as an exploration of those realms of the mind, having *seen* the ground of the mind first. The other, Tibetan Buddhism, works by the process of ten or fifteen years of going *down* bit by bit, till the ground of consciousness is reached, and then coming up swiftly. So that ulti-

mately they arrive at the same place, but the Zen method is the reverse of the Tibetan."

8 (p. 114) For Snyder's views on primitive cultures see, too, his statement to Michael and Jan Castro, *River Styx,* 4 (1979), 36: "Looking back and sideways and around the corner into what the primitive represents provides us with the only empirical alternative models, actually, to what civilization represents, and from inside civilization, we get some of the same echoes of what the possibilities might be. They can be summed up, actually, in one phrase or equation: Are you in business for money or are you in business for your health? . . . And what the primitive world has to offer [is that] it measures us in terms of final physical and psychological health."

9 (p. 133) Probably the most important work Snyder saw for the California Arts Council during his tenure lay in two areas: 1) in funding artists and programs that would bring art into communities, not as a one-time gala production but as a day-to-day part of peoples' lives, and 2) in giving real meaning to "the word 'California' in the term California Arts Council."

Snyder addressed the second of these issues in a brief correspondence with Robert Commanday of the *San Francisco Chronicle.* In a letter (February 7, 1978) addressing the validity of granting Council money to projects delving into Chicano and Native American cultural history, Snyder wrote: "It has long been known by artists that much of their inspiration and style comes from the spirit of the place. We are deeply interested in giving meaning to the word 'California' in the term California Arts Council. I know it's hard for people still accustomed to thinking with an essentially European mindset to take 'place' seriously. But one of the exciting possibilities for the future will be the rise of an artistic consciousness that has begun to draw deeply on the spirit of the place. For that reason, the many thousand year experience of Native Americans, regardless of whether they are north or south of the somewhat artificial Mexican border, will be a great instructor in certain ways of tuning into what the climatic cycles, plant and animal communities, can tell us of where we are. I know this sounds probably a trifle absurd to you, but we do already in fact live from day to day by virtue of the water, air, and agricultural productivity of the place; it is only another step to recognizing how that moves in the depths of our imaginations."

10 (p. 170) The following remarks are excerpted from two texts already cited in these notes (talks Snyder gave at San Diego State University [1973] and at Lindisfarne in New York City [1977]). They amplify in a slightly different direction Snyder's concluding discussion of poetry in "Poetry, Community & Climax" and can well serve as a preface to the final section of that talk.

On Poetry and Prose: "A few words about poetry: silence into sound, sound as we produce it with our breath, bellies, vocal chords; vertebrate, primate call, inheritance calls, into speech; living a lifetime surrounded by speech, from age one-and-a-half till the minute you die—last words—final comments. The human realm is filled up with speech. So what people call literature—to make basic distinctions—is a variety of utterance.

"Of human utterances there are two types: those that are forgotten and those that are remembered. Those that are remembered are notable, so we can say that literature is notable utterances. The span of time of the existence of literature, thus defined, can be anywhere from that of a mayfly—twenty minutes—to, concretely speaking, maybe 25,000 years, what we have some evidence of. A twenty-five minute piece of literature is a joke I tell you, you tell somebody else and then you forget it, and then they forget it. But it had that little existence, just for a bit. Volkswagen manuals, telephone books, are all literature; they're all notable utterances, they have been saved. Of the flow of speech that is all around us, some little chunks of it, a very tiny percentage, have been saved, temporarily, put aside, kept trapped. In Africa, when Frobenius was working with some African people, they asked him what he was doing

181

when he was writing, and he started to explain it to them, but before he had even gotten through the second sentence they said, 'Oh, you're trapping our words'—word trapping.

"So in the realm of speech and, shall we say, in the realm of notable utterances, there are two types: one is spoken and the other is song. Speaking is prose, plain speech; singing is poetry, poetry is song. Now you don't want to get caught up in your sense of song as just a short melodic lyric; you have to understand song in a larger picture as chanting, chanson, *cantare*. It is a way of using the voice, and usually it is a more intensified gathering of the already existing internal possibilities of the spoken language, intensifying, clarifying and presenting what are the rhythmic and phonemic possibilities of the existing natural spoken language, bringing it before your ear more sharply. Thus, Buddhist sutra chanting or religious offices of the old style mass, or the Eastern church, are poetry, singing, drama, ritual, just as a great deal of the world's drama was and is sung, poetic drama.

"Within song there are two categories. One is sacred and the other is secular. I've described already by mentioning chanting some of the sacred songs. The secular songs have been with us from the beginning. There's no place in the world that you can't find, in every culture—four thousand of them, say, four thousand different languages, 40,000 years of it—that you can't find these songs being sung, at one time or another, by everyone at some point in his or her life."

On sacred song: "On the side of sacred song, you can make two divisions. One division consists of those songs using unintelligible language, another of those using intelligible language. Most sacred songs are composed of magical words which no one knows the literal meaning of, or perhaps only a small priestly class, but the people at large do not know the literal meaning of them. Having the Roman Catholic services in Latin adds to the magic for most people. Many different traditional religions utilize archaic languages in their services for the magical power of this unintelligibility.

"In the case of, say, Hinduism and Buddhism, which I know best, we have Mantras, and we have Dhāranīs. Mantras are little short magical songs which are part translatable, but in part perhaps not; famous example: *Om Mani Padme Hūm: Om,* magical seed syllable, *Mani,* translatable word meaning jewel, *Padme,* translatable word meaning 'in the Lotus,' *Hūm,* nontranslatable word indicating victory. *Om* and *Hūm* are what you call seed syllables. They are not part of any regular language construction. They are used only in special context. In magical Sanskrit, there are a number of what are called 'seed syllables,' which are theoretically the building blocks of all languages in Sanskrit language theory, and are used sometimes all by themselves, sometimes in mixture with nonwords to create the Mantras, which are magical power, meditation phrase songs, with many different uses from the sublime to getting your enemies away, and winning girl friends.

"Another class of Sanskrit-derived magical language is to be found in the Dhāranīs. The Dhāranīs are virtually untranslatable. They are theoretically from or in Sanskrit but nobody has ever known what they meant in any culture.

"These texts contain 'magical language'—they are song, and by some definitions poetry. It's a kind of poetry, a kind of sacred poetry. That's what we're trying to expand; that's how I'm trying to expand my understanding of literature, to be able to merge and to encompass these different directions and see how they tend, in some ways, to fit together."

INDEX

185